C++ Interview Questions with Solutions

Including C++11

C++ INTERVIEW QUESTIONS WITH SOLUTIONS

Including C++11

Lin Quan

ISBN-13: 978-1489516718
ISBN-10: 1489516719

Preface

This book contains more than **200** C++ questions most frequently asked in technical interviews @top-notch software companies like Google, Microsoft, Amazon and Facebook. Detailed solutions are provided for all of these, including C++11.

For suggestions, feedback and comments, please contact :
lin.quan.20@gmail.com

Lin Quan
Retired Professor(Computer Science)
May 20, 2013

List of Chapters

List of Programs

Chapter 1

General

** Question 1   Bit-fields and Concurrency

Which of the following data members are safe for concurrent updates ?

Program 1.1: Bit-fields and Concurrency

```
1 struct A
2 {
3     char non_bitfield_a;
4
5     int bitfield_b :    3;
6     int bitfield_c :   10;
7     int     :    0;
8
9     int bitfield_d :    8;
10
11    struct E
12    {
13        int bitfield_a1 :   8;
14    } non_bitfield_e;
15
16    int bitfield_f :    4;
17    int non_bitfield_g;
18    int bitfield_h :   11;
19 };
```

Solution of Question 1

As far as concurrent update is concerned, it is related to *memory location*, i.e., two threads of execution can safely update and access *separate* memory locations.

So let us try understanding the memory location of the member data, starting with bit-fields.

Program 1.2: Bit-fields and Concurrency

```
1  struct A
2  {
3      char non_bitfield_a;
4
5      int bitfield_b  :   3;
6      int bitfield_c  :  10;
7      int      :   0;
8
9      int bitfield_d  :   8;
10
11     struct E
12     {
13         int bitfield_a1  :  8;
14     } non_bitfield_e;
15
16     int bitfield_f  :   4;
17     int non_bitfield_g;
18     int bitfield_h  :  11;
19 };
```

Concurrent Safe bit-fields

Two bit-fields are safe for concurrent updates by two threads, if they are located in separate memory locations

- *bitfield_b* and *bitfield_c* are located in the *same* memory location, hence **not thread-safe** for concurrent updates.

- *bitfield_c* and *bitfield_d* are located in *different* memory locations because these are separated by a *zero-length* bit-field, hence thread-safe for concurrent updates.

- *bitfield_d* and *bitfield_a1* are located in *different* memory locations because *bitfield_a1* is inside the nested structure *E*, hence thread-safe for concurrent updates.

- *bitfield_f* and *bitfield_h* are located in *different* memory locations because these are separated by a *non-bitfield* data member *non_bitfield_g*, hence thread-safe for concurrent updates.

Hence it is not safe to concurrently update two bit-fields in the same struct if all fields between them are also bit-fields of non-zero width because these constitute the *same* memory location.

There are seven memory locations associated with the structure *A*

1. *non_bitfield_a*

2. *bitfield_b* and *bitfield_c*

3. *bitfield_d*

4. *bitfield_a1* (*non_bitfield_e*)

5. *bitfield_f*

6. *non_bitfield_g*

7. *bitfield_h*

* Question 2   Distinct Address Location

What happens when the program below is compiled ?

Program 1.3: Distinct Address Location

```
int main()
{
    char a = 'a';
    char b = 'b';

    static_assert(&a == &b, "Address of a and
     b"
                            "should be
                            distinct");
}
```

Solution of Question 2

It results into a compilation error as enlisted below:

```
distinct_add.cpp: In function 'int main()':
distinct_add.cpp:6:5:
error: static assertion failed:
Address of a and b should be distinct
     static_assert(&a == &b, "Address of a and b "
     ^
```

Address location of two distinct objects is always distinct except when the following is true in which case the result is implementation-defined:

1. These are bit-fields

2. These are base-class sub-objects of zero size

The address of an object the address of the first byte it occupies except when it is either a bit-field or a base class sub-object of zero size.

** Question 3   Signal and Values

List the types of the objects whose values are guaranteed to be defined even in case of signals ?

Solution of Question 3

1. volatile *std::sig_atomic_t*

2. lock-free atomic objects

** Question 4   Temporary and Conversions

In the program below, what happens before temporary gets destroyed in line 12

Program 1.4: Temporary and Conversions

```
1 struct A
2 {
3     A( int  x)  :  _x(x)  {}
4
5     int  &  val ()  {  return  _x;  }
6 private :
7     int  _x;
8 };
9
10 int  main ()
11 {
12     if (A(1). val ())
13       {}
14 }
```

Solution of Question 4

The following conversion takes place before destruction of the temporary object of type *A*

1. lvalue to rvalue conversion

2. int to bool conversion

** Question 5   evaluation of expressions

Review the program below:

Program 1.5: evaluation of expressions

```
 1 void compute(int, int) {};
 2
 3 void eval(int x, int arr[])
 4 {
 5     x = arr[x++];
 6
 7     x = 2, x++, x++;
 8
 9     x = x++ + 1;
10     x = x + 1;
11
12     compute(x = -1, x = -1);
13 }
```

Solution of Question 5

- line 5: behavior is undefined

- line 7: x becomes 4

- line 9: behavior is undefined

- line 10: the value of x is incremented

- line 12: behavior is undefined

*** Question 6   trigraph sequences

What happens with the trigraphs here:

Program 1.6: trigraph sequences

```
 1 ??=define validateArray(x, y) x??(y??)  ??!??!
     y??(x??)
```

Solution of Question 6

- trigraph ??= is replaced by #

- trigraph ??(is replaced by [

- trigraph ??) is replaced by]

- trigraph ??! is replaced by |

The above $\Longrightarrow$ that the stated trigraph sequences will be replaced to change the expression to look like below

Program 1.7: replacing trigraph sequences
```
1 #define validateArray(x, y) x[y] || y[x]
```

** Question 7   increment operator

What is the output of the program:

Program 1.8: increment operator
```
1 #include <iostream>
2
3 int main()
4 {
5     int one = 1;
6     int two = 2;
7
8     int a = one+++++two;
9 }
```

Solution of Question 7

When compiled, the error is:

```
increment_operator.cpp: In function 'int main()':
increment_operator.cpp:8:18:
error: lvalue required as increment operand
     int a = one+++++two;
                  ^
```

The expression *one+++++two* is parsed to look like *one ++ ++ + two*, which violates a constraint on increment operators, thus leading to incorrect expression.

$$one{+}{+}{+}{+}{+}two \Longrightarrow one \; {+}{+} \; {+}{+} \; {+} \; two$$

Please note that the expression *one+++++two* is not parsed as
one ++ + ++ two, which is indeed a correct expression.

$$one{+}{+}{+}{+}{+}two \;\not\Rightarrow\; one \;{+}{+} \;{+} \;{+}{+}\; two$$

* Question 8   nullptr

What is *nullptr* ?

Solution of Question 8

nullptr is the *pointer literal* designating a *prvalue* of type *std::nullptr_t*. It is a null pointer constant which can be converted to a null pointer value or a null member pointer value. Please note that *std::nullptr_t* itself

• is not a pointer type

• is not a pointer to member type

• is a *distinct type*

** Question 9   user defined literal

What is *user defined literal* ?

Solution of Question 9

A *user defined literal* is a call to a literal operator or literal operator template of the form

1. operator "" *identifier*

2. operator "" *identifier*$<$'c_1', 'c_2', ... 'c_k'$>()$

For example:

1. *user-defined-integer-literal*

   a) operator "" *identifier* (n ULL)

   b) operator "" *identifier* ("n")

   c) operator "" *identifier* $<$'c_1', 'c_2', ... 'c_k'$>()$

2. *user-defined-floating-literal*

   a) operator "" *identifier* (f L)

   b) operator "" *identifier* ("f")

   c) operator "" *identifier* $<$'c_1', 'c_2', ... 'c_k'$>()$

3. *user-defined-string-literal*

a) operator "" *identifier* (str, len)

b) operator "" *identifier* (ch)

Program 1.9: user defined literal

```
1 #include <string>
2
3 void operator "" _distance(long double);
4
5 long double operator "" _amount(long double);
6
7 std::string operator "" _amount(const
      char16_t*,
8                                      std::size_t);
9
10 unsigned     operator "" _amount(const char*);
11
12 float operator "" _X(const char*);
13
14 template <char...> int operator "" _length();
15
16 int main()
17 {
18     2.9_amount;
19
20     u"test"_amount;
21
22     20_amount;
23 }
```

In the example above

- line 18 calls *operator* "" _amount(2.9L)

- line 20 calls *operator* "" _amount(u"test", 4)

- line 22 calls *operator* "" _amount("20")

* Question 10   Declaration vs Definition

Which of the following are definitions and which are just declarations?

Program 1.10: Declaration vs Definition

```
1 extern int a1;
2 int a2;
3 extern const int a3;
4 extern const int a4 = 10;
5 void fun(int);
```

```
 6 void fun(int i) {}
 7 struct A;
 8 struct A
 9 {
10      int x, y;
11 };
12 typedef int Integer;
13 enum {low, mid, high};
14 extern A _A;
15 struct B
16 {
17      static int x;
18 };
19 int B::x = 5;
20 namespace Detail { int x; }
21 using Detail::x;
22 namespace DetailsX = Detail;
23 B b1;
```

Solution of Question 10

- *Declarations*
  line 1, 3, 5, 7, 12, 14, 17, 21

- *Definitions*
  Rest are definitions

** Question 11   Compiler Generated Member Functions

In the following case, list the member functions whose definitions are implicitly generated by the compiler :

Program 1.11: Sample Class

```
 1 #include <string>
 2
 3 struct A
 4 {
 5      std::string _str;
 6 };
 7
 8 int main()
 9 {
10      A a1;
11      A a2 = a1;
12      a2 = a1;
13 };
```

Solution of Question 11

The following member functions definitions are implicitly generated by the compiler:

1. default constructor

```
A() : _str() { }
```

2. copy constructor

```
A(const A & a): _str(a._str) { }
```

3. move constructor

```
A(A&& a)
:
_str(static_cast<std::string&&>(a._str))
{ }
```

or,

```
A(A&& a)
:
_str(std::move(a._str)) { }
```

4. copy assignment operator

```
A& operator=(const A& a)
{
    _str = a._str;
    return *this;
}
```

5. move assignment operator

```
A& operator=(A&& a)
{
    _str =
    static_cast<std::string&&>(a._str);
    return *this;
}
```

or,

```
A& operator=(A&& a)
{
    _str = std::move(a._str);
    return *this;
}
```

6. destructor

```
~A() { }
```

Hence it may look like :

Program 1.12: Compiler Generated Member Functions

```
1 #include <string>
2
3 struct A
```

```
 4 {
 5      std :: string _str ;
 6
 7      A() : _str () { }
 8
 9      A(const A & a): _str(a._str) { }
10
11      A(A&& a)
12      :
13      _str(static_cast<std :: string&&>(a._str))
          { }
14
15      A& operator=(const A& a)
16      {
17          _str = a._str;
18          return *this;
19      }
20
21      A& operator=(A&& a)
22      {
23          _str = static_cast<std :: string&&>(a.
              _str);
24          return *this;
25      }
26
27      ~A() { }
28 };
```

or,

Program 1.13: Compiler Generated Member Functions

```
 1 #include <string>
 2
 3 struct A
 4 {
 5      std :: string _str ;
 6
 7      A() : _str () { }
 8
 9      A(const A & a): _str(a._str) { }
10
11      A(A&& a)
12      :
13      _str(std :: move(a._str)) { }
14
15      A& operator=(const A& a)
16      {
17          _str = a._str;
18          return *this;
19      }
20
```

```
21      A& operator=(A&& a)
22      {
23          _str = std::move(a._str);
24          return *this;
25      }
26
27      ~A() { }
28 };
```

*** Question 12   ODR vs Default Constructor

What is the output of these two programs?

Program 1.14: ODR vs Default Constructor

```
1 #include <iostream>
2
3 struct Base
4 {
5      Base(int);
6
7      Base(int, int);
8 };
9
10 Base::Base(int = 0)
11 {
12      std::cout << "Inside Base::Base(int)"
13                << std::endl;
14 }
15
16 struct Derived : Base
17 {
18 };
19
20 int main()
21 {
22      Derived d;
23 }
```

Program 1.15: ODR vs Default Constructor

```
1 #include <iostream>
2
3 struct Base
4 {
5      Base(int);
6
7      Base(int, int);
8 };
9
```

```
10 Base :: Base ( int = 0 , int = 0)
11 {
12     std :: cout << "Inside Base :: Base ( int , int )
       "
13                     << std :: endl ;
14 }
15
16 struct Derived : Base
17 {
18 };
19
20 int main ()
21 {
22     Derived d;
23 }
```

Solution of Question 12

In the first program, the output is *Inside Base::Base(int)*

In the second program, the output is *Inside Base::Base(int, int)*

In both of these programs, the class Derived's default constructor is implicitly defined, but this definition D() calls Base(int) in one case and calls Base(int, int) in another case.

** Question 13   Understanding Point of Declaration

What is the output of this program? How the template arguments are deduced for the class template B?

Program 1.16: Understanding Point of Declaration

```
1 #include <iostream>
2
3 void test ()
4 {
5     int a1 = 10;
6     {
7         int a1 = a1;
8         std :: cout << "a1: " << a1
9                     << std :: endl ;
10     }
11
12     const int a2 = 20;
13     {
14         int a2 [a2];
15         std :: cout << "size of array:"
16             << sizeof(a2)/sizeof(int)
```

```
17                    << std :: endl ;
18        }
19
20     const int a3 = 30;
21     {
22          enum { a3 = a3 };
23          std :: cout << "enum␣a3␣is :␣"
24                    << a3 << std :: endl ;
25     }
26 }
27
28 struct A
29 {
30     enum { e = 40 };
31
32     int arr [A :: e ];
33 };
34
35 typedef int T;
36
37 template<typename T = T, T n = 0>
38 struct B{};
39
40 int main ()
41 {
42     test ();
43
44     A a;
45     std :: cout << "length␣of␣array␣arr␣is␣:"
46                 << sizeof (a . arr )/ sizeof (int )
47                 << std :: endl ;
48 }
```

Solution of Question 13

The output is

```
a1: 6295552
size of array:20
enum a3 is: 30
length of array arr is :40
```

Please note that:

- Value of the second integer a1 is initialized with its own value which is indeterminate.

- The first template argument's default value type is looked
  up to find the typedef int and in the case of the second
  one, look up finds the template parameter.

** Question 14   class scope variables

What is the output of this program?

Program 1.17: class scope variables

```
1 #include <cstddef>
2 #include <iostream>
3
4 typedef int c;
5
6 enum { e = 10 };
7
8 struct A
9 {
10     char arr[e];
11
12     std::size_t fun()
13     {
14         return sizeof(c);
15     }
16
17     char c;
18
19     enum { e = 20 };
20 };
21
22 int main()
23 {
24     A a;
25     std::cout << "size of arr is :"
26         << sizeof(a.arr)/sizeof(char)
27         << std::endl;
28
29     std::cout << "fun() :" << a.fun()
30             << std::endl;
31 }
```

Solution of Question 14

The output is

```
size of arr is :10
fun() :1
```

** Question 15   namespace scope variables

What is the output of this program?

Program 1.18: namespace scope variables

```
 1 namespace A
 2 {
 3     int  i ;
 4
 5     int  func ( int  j )
 6     {
 7         return  j ;
 8     }
 9
10     int  g ( ) ;
11
12     void  h ( ) ;
13 }
14
15 namespace
16 {
17     int  x = 10;
18 }
19
20 namespace A
21 {
22     int  func ( char  j )
23     {
24         return  x + j ;
25     }
26
27     int  i ;
28
29     int  g ( ) ;
30
31     int  g ( )
32     {
33         return  func ( i ) ;
34     }
35
36     int  h ( ) ;
37 }
```

Solution of Question 15

The output is

```
namespace_scope.cpp:27:9:
```

```
error: redefinition of 'i'
    int i;
      ^

namespace_scope.cpp:3:9:
note: previous definition is here
    int i;
      ^

namespace_scope.cpp:36:9:
error: functions that differ only
in their return type cannot be overloaded
    int h();
      ^

namespace_scope.cpp:12:10:
note: previous declaration is
here
    void h();
       ^

2 errors generated.
```

Please note that

- the potential scope of the variable x on line 17 in the unnamed namespace is to the end of the translation unit.

- line 22 overloads A::func(int)

- line 24 : x is from the anonymous namespace

- line 27 redefines int i : violation of ODR(One Definition Rule) : Hence *error*.

- line 29 re-declares the function g()

- line 31 : defines the function g()

- line 33 : calls A::func(int)

- line 36 : redefines the function h() with different return type: hence *error*.

** Question 16   scope of template parameters

Can a template parameter be used in the declaration of subsequent template parameters and their default arguments ?

Solution of Question 16

Yes.

A template parameter be used in the declaration of subsequent template parameters and and their default arguments.

For example,

```
1 template<typename T1, T1* ptr, typename T2 =
    T1>
2 struct A {};
3
4 template<typename T> void alloc_memory(T* ptr
    = new T);
```

Please note that a template parameter can be used also in the specification of base classes, like

```
1 template<typename T>
2 struct Base {};
3
4 template<typename T>
5 struct Derived : Base<T> { };
6
7 template<typename T>
8 struct A : T { };
```

The use of a template parameter as a base class implies that a class used as a template argument must be defined and not just declared when the class template is instantiated.

** Question 17   scope of template parameters

What is the type of the template parameters T1 and T2 in the program below ?

```
1 typedef int T;
2
3 template<T T1, typename T, template<T T2>
    class T3>
4 struct A;
```

Solution of Question 17

- T1 is a non-type template parameter of type int

- T2 is a non-type template parameter of the same type as the second template parameter of A.

** Question 18   Unqualified Name Lookup

What is the output of the program ?

Program 1.19: Unqualified Name Lookup

```cpp
#include <iostream>

typedef int func;

namespace A
{
    struct B
    {
        B(int i = 1) : _i(i) {}

        friend void func(B & b)
        {
            std::cout << "func()" << std::endl;
        }

        operator int() { return _i; }

        void compute(B b)
        {
            _i = func(b);
        }
    private:
        int _i;
    }; // struct B
} // namespace A

int main()
{
    A::B b1(10), b2(20);

    std::cout << b2 << std::endl;

    b2.compute(b1);

    std::cout << b2 << std::endl;
}
```

Solution of Question 18

The output is:

```
20
10
```

Please note that on line 20, *func* is not a function call, hence the argument dependent lookup does not apply and the friend function *func* is not found.

Hence it is equivalent to a call to *int(b)*.

** Question 19   Unqualified Name Lookup

What is the output of the program ?

Program 1.20: Unqualified Name Lookup

```cpp
#include <iostream>

int a = 10;

namespace outer
{
    int a = 20;

    namespace inner
    {
        int a = 30;

        void func ();
    } // namespace inner
} // namespace outer


void outer :: inner :: func ()
{
    // int a = 40;
    std :: cout << "a : " << a << std :: endl;
}

int main ()
{
    outer :: inner :: func ();
}
```

Discuss how the declaration of the variable *a* is being looked up when trying to use it within definition of the function *func*.

Solution of Question 19

The output is:

```
a : 30
```

The following scopes are searched in the given order for a declaration/definition of the variable *a*:

1. the first is the outermost block scope of outer::inner::func, before the use of *a*, i.e., if line number 20 is commented out, then it is the first place where lookup is done. In this case the output will be *40*.

2. next is the scope of the namespace inner(line number 11), as illustrated by the output being *30*.

3. next is the scope of the namespace outer, i.e., if the line numbers 20 and 11 do not declare/define *a* then due to line 7, the output will be 20.

4. next is the global scope, before the definition of outer::inner::func, i.e., if line numbers 20, 11 and 7 do not declare/define *a* then due to line 3, the output will be 10.

** Question 20   Unqualified Name Lookup

What is the output of the program ?

Program 1.21: Unqualified Name Lookup

```
1 #include <iostream>
2
3 namespace first
4 {
5     struct base
6     {
7         static int i;
8     };
9 } // namespace A
10
11 int first::base::i = 10;
12
13 namespace second
14 {
15     struct derived : first::base
16     {
17         struct nested
18         {
19             nested()
20             {
21                 std::cout << "nested() : "
22                     << i << std::endl;
23             }
24         } n; // struct nested
25     }; // struct derived
26 }
```

```
27
28 int  main ( )
29 {
30      second :: derived  d ;
31 }
```

Discuss how the declaration of the variable i is being looked up when trying to use it during constructor definition of *nested*.

Solution of Question 20

The output is:

```
nested()  :  10
```

The following scopes are searched in the given order for a declaration/definition of the variable i:

1. scope of struct second::derived::nested, before the use of i

2. scope of struct second::derived, before the definition of second::derived::nested

3. scope of second::derived's base class first::base(as given in the program)

4. scope of namespace second, before the definition of second::derived

5. global scope, before the definition of second

* Question 21   Unqualified Name Lookup

What is the output of the program ?

Program 1.22: Unqualified Name Lookup

```
1 struct  Base  { };
2
3 namespace  outer
4 {
5      namespace  inner
6      {
7           struct  Derived  :  Base
8           {
9                void  func ( ) ;
10           }; // struct  Derived
```

```
11      } // namespace inner
12 } // namespace outer
13
14 void outer :: inner :: Derived :: func ()
15 {
16      i = 10;
17 }
```

Discuss how the declaration of the variable *i* is being looked up when trying to use it within *outer::inner::Derived::func*.

Solution of Question 21

The following scopes are searched in the given order for a declaration/definition of the variable *i*:

1. outermost block scope of outer::inner::Derived::func, before the use of i

2. scope of struct outer::inner::Derived

3. scope of outer::inner::Derived's base class B

4. scope of namespace outer::inner

5. scope of namespace outer

6. global scope, before the definition of outer::inner::Derived::func

*** Question 22   Friend member func vs Name-Lookup

What are the parameter types of the friend functions *f* and *g* and template argument of the friend function template*h* (on line numbers 18, 20 and 22 respectively) ?

Program 1.23: Friend member function and Name Lookup

```
1 struct A
2 {
3      typedef int AType;
4
5      void f (AType);
6
7      void g(float);
8
9      template <typename T> void h();
10 };
11
12 struct B
```

```
13 {
14      typedef char AType;
15
16      typedef float BType;
17
18      friend void A:: f (AType) ;
19
20      friend void A:: g (BType) ;
21
22      friend void A:: h<AType>() ;
23 };
```

Solution of Question 22

```
friend void A::f(AType);
```

It is first looked up in the scope of the member function's class
A.
Hence the parameter type is *A::AType*.

```
friend void A::g(BType);
```

It is not found in the scope of the member function's class *A*,
hence the look up is done in the scope of the class granting
friendship, i.e., *B*.
Hence the parameter type is *B::BType*.

```
friend void A::h<AType>();
```

Because the name is part of a template-argument in the declarator-
id, hence it is looked up in the scope of the class granting friendship, i.e., *B*.
Hence the template argument is *B::AType*.

*** Question 23   namespace extern and look-up

What is the output of the program?

Program 1.24: namespace extern and look-up
```
1 #include <iostream>
2
```

```
3 namespace A
4 {
5      int x = 10;
6
7      extern int y;
8 } // namespace A
9
10 int x = 20;
11
12 int A::y = x;
13
14 int main()
15 {
16     std::cout << "A::y is : "
17             << A::y << std::endl;
18 }
```

Solution of Question 23

The output is:

```
A::y is : 10
```

Because the variable member *y* of the namespace *A* is defined outside the scope of its namespace, that's why look up of the variable *x* occurs in the same way when *y* could have been defined inside the namespace.

Hence the un-qualified look-up of *x* in the definition of *y* is interpreted as *A::x*.

*** Question 24   ADL(Argument Dependent Look-up)

What is the output of the program?

Program 1.25: ADL

```
1 #include <iostream>
2
3 struct B {};
4
5 namespace A
6 {
7      struct B {};
8
9      void func(B b)
10     {
11          std::cout << "A::func" << std::endl;
12     }
```

```
13 } // namespace A
14
15 void func (B b)
16 {
17     std :: cout << "func" << std :: endl;
18 }
19
20 void test ()
21 {
22     A::B b1;
23
24     func (b1);
25
26     B b2;
27
28     func (b2);
29 }
30
31 int main ()
32 {
33     test ();
34 }
```

Solution of Question 24

The output is:

```
A::func
func
```

Please note that unqualified *func* resulted into a look-up into the namespace *A* because the type of the argument *A::B* being passed to the function *func* is defined in that namespace.

This is also known as ADL, i.e., Argument Dependent Look-up or Koenig's name look-up.

*** **Question 25**   **ADL(Argument Dependent Look-up)**

What is the output of the program?

Program 1.26: ADL

```
1 #include <iostream>
2
3 namespace A
4 {
5     struct B {};
6
```

```
7       void func(B b)
8       {
9           std::cout << "A::func" << std::endl;
10      }
11 } // namespace A
12
13 void func(A::B b)
14 {
15     std::cout << "func(A::B)" << std::endl;
16 }
17
18 void test()
19 {
20     A::B b1;
21
22     func(b1);
23 }
24
25 int main()
26 {
27     test();
28 }
```

Solution of Question 25

The program doesn't get compiled. Compiler error is:

```
adl2.cpp:22:5: error: call to 'func' is ambiguous
    func(b1);
    ^~~~
adl2.cpp:7:10: note: candidate function
    void func(B b)
         ^
adl2.cpp:13:6: note: candidate function
void func(A::B b)
     ^

1 error generated.
```

It is self-explanatory from the compiler error.

**** Question 26   ADL(Argument Dependent Look-up)

Modify the previous program to call *func(A::B)*?

Solution of Question 26

Modified program looks like

Program 1.27: ADL

```
1 #include <iostream>
2
3 namespace A
4 {
5     struct B {};
6
7     void func(B b)
8     {
9         std::cout << "A::func" << std::endl;
10    }
11 } // namespace A
12
13 void func(A::B b)
14 {
15    std::cout << "func(A::B)" << std::endl;
16 }
17
18 void test()
19 {
20    A::B b1;
21
22    extern void func(A::B);
23
24    func(b1);
25 }
26
27 int main()
28 {
29    test();
30 }
```

Now the output looks like

```
func(A::B)
```

** Question 27   Basic Look-up

Review the program below?

Program 1.28: Basic Look-up

```
1 struct A
2 {
3     static int a;
4 };
5
```

```
6 int  A::a  =  10;
7
8 int  main()
9 {
10      int  A  =  20;
11
12      A::a  =  100;
13
14      A  a1;
15 }
```

Solution of Question 27

This program doesn't get compiled and the compiler error is

```
basic_lookup.cpp:14:5:
error: must use 'struct' tag to refer
to type 'A' in this
      scope
    A a1;
    ^
    struct
basic_lookup.cpp:10:9:
note: struct 'A' is hidden by a
non-type declaration of
      'A' here
    int A = 20;
        ^

1 error generated.
```

The error is self-explanatory because on line 14 : A is not a type anymore.

** Question 28   Basic Look-up

Review the definition of static data member *array* below.

Program 1.29: Basic Look-up

```
1 struct  A  {  };
2
3 struct  B
4 {
5      struct  A  {  };
6
7      static  const  int  n  =  10;
```

```
8
9       static A array [n];
10 };
11
12 A B:: array [n];
```

Solution of Question 28

This program doesn't get compiled and the compiler error is

```
basic_lookup1.cpp:12:13:
error: conflicting declaration
'A B::array [10]'
 A B::array[n];
            ^

basic_lookup1.cpp:9:14:
error: 'B::array' has a previous
declaration as 'B::A B::array [10]'
     static A array[n];
              ^

basic_lookup1.cpp:12:13: error: declaration of
'B::A B::array [10]'
outside of class is not definition
[-fpermissive]
 A B::array[n];
            ^
```

Another compiler's error is

```
basic_lookup1.cpp:12:6:
 error: redefinition of 'array'
with a different type:
      'A [10]' vs 'B::A [10]'
A B::array[n];
     ^

basic_lookup1.cpp:9:14:
note: previous definition is here
     static A array[n];
              ^

1 error generated.
```

The error is self-explanatory.

The following program fixes this error:

Program 1.30: Basic Look-up

```
1 struct A { };
2
3 struct B
4 {
5     struct A { };
6
7     static const int n = 10;
8
9     static A array[n];
10 };
11
12 B::A B::array[n];
```

* Question 29   destructor and typedef

How to call the destructor explicitly for the typedef of a given class ?

Solution of Question 29

The following program demonstrates it:

Program 1.31: destructor and typedef

```
1 struct B
2 {
3     ~B() {}
4 };
5
6 typedef B AnotherB;
7
8 int main()
9 {
10     AnotherB * third;
11
12     third->AnotherB::~AnotherB();
13 }
```

** Question 30   constructor name look-up

How to look-up constructors of the class *Base* in two cases : one as *Base* itself, another as a base class of *Derived* in the given program ?

```
struct Base
{
    Base();
};

struct Derived : Base
{
    Derived();
};

Base::Base() { }
Derived::Derived() { }
```

Solution of Question 30

Invocation of Base's constructor as a base part of derived will look like:

```
Derived::Base db;
```

Following the same league, the call below is not legal

```
Base::Base b;
```

because *Base::Base* doesn't name a type.

To achieve this, the following should be attempted:

```
struct Base::Base b1;
```

** Question 31   understanding namespace

Given the program below:

```
int x;

namespace Y
{
    void f(float);
    void h(int);
}

namespace Z
{
    void h(double);
}

namespace A
{
    using namespace Y;

    void f(int);
    void g(int);

    int i;
}

namespace B
{
    using namespace Z;

    void f(char);

    int i;
}

namespace AB
{
    using namespace A;
    using namespace B;

    void g();
}
```

What happens with the code fragments as follows:

1.
```
AB::g();
```

2.
```
AB::f(1);
```

3.
```
AB::f('e');
```

4.
```
AB::x++;
```

5.
```
AB::i++;
```

6.
```
AB::h(2.7);
```

Solution of Question 31

1.
```
AB::g();
```

Since g is declared directly in AB, it calls AB::g().

2.
```
AB::f(1);
```

Since f is not declared directly in AB so the rules are applied recursively to A and B; namespace Y is not searched and Y::f(float) is not considered;

So the candidate set is A::f(int), B::f(char) and overload resolution chooses A::f(int).

3.
```
AB::f('e');
```

as above but resolution chooses B::f(char).

4.
```
AB::x++;
```

Since x is not declared directly in AB, and is not declared in A or B , so the rules are applied recursively to Y and Z, hence nothing is found, so the program is ill-formed.

5.
```
AB::i++;
```

Since i is not declared directly in AB so the rules are applied recursively to A and B, so the choices are A::i , B::i so the use is ambiguous and the program is ill-formed.

6.
```
AB::h(2.7);
```

Since h is not declared directly in AB and not declared directly in A or B so the rules are applied recursively to Y and Z, so the choices are Y::h(int), Z::h(double) and overload resolution chooses Z::h(double).

** Question 32   multiple declarations are ok

Given the program below, what happens with line numbers 24 and 40 ?

Program 1.32: multiple declarations are ok

```
1 namespace A
2 {
3     int a;
4 }
```

```
 5
 6 namespace B
 7 {
 8      using namespace A;
 9 }
10
11 namespace C
12 {
13      using namespace A;
14 }
15
16 namespace BC
17 {
18      using namespace B;
19      using namespace C;
20 }
21
22 void f ()
23 {
24      BC::a++;
25 }
26
27 namespace D
28 {
29      using A::a;
30 }
31
32 namespace BD
33 {
34      using namespace B;
35      using namespace D;
36 }
37
38 void g ()
39 {
40      BD::a++;
41 }
```

Solution of Question 32

As we already know that the same declaration found more
than once is not an ambiguity at all because it is still a unique

declaration, hence the calls at the line numbers 24 and 40 are ok because both refers to *A::i*.

** Question 33   multiple references to namespace

What is the output of the program ?

Program 1.33: multiple declarations are ok

```cpp
1 #include <iostream>
2
3 namespace first
4 {
5     int one = 1;
6 }
7
8 namespace second
9 {
10     using namespace first;
11
12     int two = 2;
13 }
14
15 namespace first
16 {
17     using namespace second;
18 }
19
20 int main()
21 {
22     second::two++;
23     first::two++;
24     second::one++;
25     first::one++;
26
27     std::cout << "first::one is "
28     << first::one << std::endl;
29
30     std::cout << "second::one is "
31     << second::one << std::endl;
32
33     std::cout << "first::two is "
34     << first::two << std::endl;
35
36     std::cout << "second::two is "
37     << second::two << std::endl;
38 }
```

Solution of Question 33

Because each referenced namespace is searched at most once, that's why the out of the program is :

```
first::one is 3
second::one is 3
first::two is 4
second::two is 4
```

** Question 34   non-type name and namespace

Review the program ?

Program 1.34: non-type name and namespace

```
1 namespace A
2 {
3     struct x {};
4
5     int x;
6     int y;
7 } // namespace A
8
9 namespace B
10 {
11     struct y {};
12 } // namespace B
13
14 namespace C
15 {
16     using namespace A;
17     using namespace B;
18
19     int i = C::x;
20     int j = C::y;
21 } // namespace C
```

Solution of Question 34

The program doesn't get compiled, the compiler error is

```
namespace3.cpp:20:16:
error: a type named 'y' is hidden
by a declaration in a
        different namespace
    int j = C::y;
        ~~~^
```

```
namespace3.cpp:11:12:
note: type declaration hidden
    struct y {};
         ^

namespace3.cpp:6:9:
note: declaration hides type
    int y;
       ^

1 error generated.
```

Please note that the non-type name hides the class or enumeration name if and only if the declarations are from the same namespace .

Hence *int i = C::x;* is a call to *A::x* of type int.

int j = C::y; is ambiguous, *A::y* or *B::y.*

** Question 35   declaration and nested namespace

Is the following definition of the function *func* is correct ?

Program 1.35: declaration and nested namespace

```
1 #include <iostream>
2
3 namespace A
4 {
5     namespace B
6     {
7         void func();
8     } // namespace B
9
10    using namespace B;
11 } // namespace A
12
13 void A::func() {}
```

Solution of Question 35

The program doesn't get compiled, the compiler error is

```
nested_namespace.cpp:13:9:
error: out-of-line definition of
'func' does not
     match any declaration in namespace 'A'
```

```
void A::func() {}
       ^~~~
1 error generated.
```

Another compiler's error is

```
nested_namespace.cpp:13:14:
error: 'void A::B::func()'
should have been declared inside 'A'
 void A::func() {}
        ^
```

Because *func* is not a member of *A*, that's why this is in error. To correct it, the program may be modified to look like:

Program 1.36: declaration and nested namespace

```
1 #include <iostream>
2
3 namespace A
4 {
5     namespace B
6     {
7         void func();
8     } // namespace B
9
10    using namespace B;
11 } // namespace A
12
13 using namespace A;
14
15 void B::func() {}
```

So qualifying with *::* is strictly applicable to direct belonging of a member to that scope.

In this case, we can even drop the *::* for defining it like:

Program 1.37: declaration and nested namespace

```
1 #include <iostream>
2
3 namespace A
4 {
5     namespace B
6     {
7         void func();
8     } // namespace B
```

```
 9
10      using namespace B;
11 } // namespace A
12
13 using namespace A;
14
15 void func () {}
```

* Question 36   declaration : global vs local

What is the difference between these two programs ?

```
struct A
{
    struct B * b;
};
```

```
struct A
{
    B * b;
};
```

Solution of Question 36

```
struct A
{
    struct B * b;
};
```

declares a struct B at global scope, i.e., the program below is valid as well

```
struct A
{
    struct B * b;
};

B *b1;
```

Whereas the program below is trying to use a not yet declared type *B*:

```
struct A
{
    B * b;
};
```

Hence it doesn't compile.

** Question 37   injected class name

What is the output of the program ?

Program 1.38: injected class name

```
 1 #include <iostream>
 2
 3 struct A
 4 {
 5     A()
 6     {
 7         std::cout << "::A()" << std::endl;
 8     }
 9
10     ~A()
11     {
12         std::cout << "::~A()" << std::endl;
13     }
14 };
15
16 struct B
17 {
18     struct A
19     {
20         A()
21         {
22             std::cout << "B::A()" << std::
                 endl;
23         }
24
25         ~A()
26         {
27             std::cout << "B::~A()" << std::
                 endl;
28         }
```

```
29      };
30
31      void  f ( ::A*  a ) ;
32 };
33
34 void  B:: f ( ::A*  a )
35 {
36      a−>~A ( ) ;
37 }
38
39 int  main ( )
40 {
41      B( ) . f ( new  A ) ;
42 }
```

Solution of Question 37

The output is:

```
::A()
::~A()
```

Because lookup in *a on line number 36 finds the injected-class-name *::A*.

** Question 38   linkage

What is linkage ?

Solution of Question 38

When a name, introduced by a declaration in another scope, related to anyone of the following refers to the same

- object

- reference

- function

- type

- template

- namespace

- value

then it is said to have a *linkage*.

There are two types of linkages:

1. *external linkage*

   When a name denotes an entity which can be referred to by names from either of these units

   a) scopes of other translation units, or

   b) other scopes of the same translation unit,

   then it is said to have an *external linkage*.

   For example

   - the name of a variable declared by a block scope *extern* declaration.

   - a member function, static data member, a named class or enumeration of class scope, or an unnamed class or enumeration defined in a class-scope typedef declaration such that the class or enumeration has the typedef name for linkage purposes, has external linkage if the name of the class has external linkage.

   - All namespaces except an unnamed namespace or a namespace declared directly or indirectly within an unnamed namespace.

2. *internal linkage*

   When a name denotes an entity which can be referred to by names only from other scopes of the same translation unit, then it is said to have an *internal linkage*.

   For example

   - *static* variable, function or function template in a namespace scope

   - *const* or *constexpr* variable without any explicit *extern* declaration.

   - anonymous union's data members.

   - An unnamed namespace or a namespace declared directly or indirectly within an unnamed namespace.

When the entity denoted by a given name cannot be referred to by names from other scopes, then that name is said is to have *no linkage*.

* Question 39 return from main

What is the significance of return statement from the *main* function?

Solution of Question 39

A return statement in *main* has the effect of

1. leaving the main function

2. destroying any objects with automatic storage duration and

3. calling std::exit with the return value as the argument.

If control reaches the end of *main* without encountering a return statement, the effect is that of executing *return 0*;

*** Question 40 static and std::atexit

What is the output of the program ?

Program 1.39: static and std::atexit

```cpp
#include <cstdlib>
#include <iostream>

struct A
{
    A()
    {
        std::cout << "A()" << std::endl;
    }
    ~A()
    {
        std::cout << "~A()" << std::endl;
    }
};

static A a;

void func()
{
    std::cout << "func()" << std::endl;
}

int main()
{
    std::atexit(&func);
}
```

Solution of Question 40

Output of the program is:

```
A()
func()
~A()
```

Please note that here static object *a* is initialized before entry to the main function and registration of function *func* with *std::atexit* happens after this. Hence *func* is called before destruction of the static object *a*.

*** Question 41   std::atexit and static

What is the output of the program ?

Program 1.40: std::atexit and static

```cpp
#include <cstdlib>
#include <iostream>

struct A
{
    A()
    {
        std::cout << "A()" << std::endl;
    }
    ~A()
    {
        std::cout << "~A()" << std::endl;
    }
};

void func()
{
    std::cout << "func()" << std::endl;
}

struct B
{
    B()
    {
        std::cout << "B()" << std::endl;
        std::atexit(&func);
    }
    ~B()
```

```
29      {
30              std :: cout <<  "~B()" << std :: endl;
31      }
32
33 };
34
35 static B b;
36
37 static A a;
38
39 int  main ()
40 {
41 }
```

Solution of Question 41

Output of the program is:

```
B()
A()
~A()
~B()
func()
```

Please note that here a call to *std::atexit* is sequenced before the completion of the initialization of the object *a* with static storage duration, hence the call to the destructor for the object *a* is sequenced before the call to the function *func* passed to *std::atexit*.

In the similar manner, let us review the program below:

Program 1.41: std::atexit and static

```
1 #include <cstdlib>
2 #include <iostream>
3
4 void func ()
5 {
6      std :: cout << "func()" << std :: endl;
7 }
8
9 struct A
10 {
11      A()
12      {
13              std :: cout << "A()" << std :: endl;
```

```
14            std :: atexit (&func ) ;
15     }
16     ~A ( )
17     {
18            std :: cout << "~A ( ) " << std :: endl ;
19     }
20 } ;
21
22 static  A  a ;
23
24 int  main ( )
25 {
26 }
```

Output of this program is:

```
A()
~A()
func()
```

** Question 42   two std::atexit

What is the output of the program ?

Program 1.42: two std::atexit

```
1 #include <cstdlib>
2 #include <iostream>
3
4 void  func ( )
5 {
6      std :: cout << "func ( ) " << std :: endl ;
7 }
8
9 struct  A
10 {
11     A ( )
12     {
13            std :: cout << "A ( )" << std :: endl ;
14            std :: atexit (&func ) ;
15     }
16     ~A ( )
17     {
18            std :: cout << "~A ( ) " << std :: endl ;
19     }
20 } ;
```

```
21
22 static A a;
23
24 int  main()
25 {
26 }
```

Solution of Question 42

Output of the program is:

```
f2()
f1()
```

It is self-explanatory.

** Question 43   Storage Duration

How many types of storage duration is possible with a given object once it is created ?

Solution of Question 43

There are four types of storage duration determining the minimum potential lifetime of the storage containing the object as given below:

1. dynamic storage duration : enabled by the global allocation functions *operator new* and *operator new[]*.

2. static storage duration : enabled by *static*. The storage for these entities shall last for the duration of the program.

3. thread storage duration : enabled by *thread_local*

4. automatic storage duration : enabled by *register* or not explicitly declared *static* or *extern*.

* Question 44   Integral Types

What are integral types ?

Solution of Question 44

The following types are collectively called *Integral Types*:

- bool

- char

- char16_t

- char32_t

- wchar_t

- the signed integer types, and

- unsigned integer types

** Question 45   Integral Types

What are integral types ?

Solution of Question 45

The following types are collectively called *Integral Types*:

- bool

- char

- char16_t

- char32_t

- wchar_t

- the signed integer types, and

- unsigned integer types

** Question 46   Ordering : const/volatile

Enlist the partial ordering relations on *const* and *volatile* ?

Solution of Question 46

Please note that cv stands for const and/or volatile.

- no cv-qualifier < const

- no cv-qualifier < volatile

- no cv-qualifier < const volatile

- const < const volatile

- volatile < const volatile

*** Question 47   Value Category : lvalue/rvalue

What is lvalue ?

What is rvalue ?

Discuss other members of an expression's value category.

Solution of Question 47

The hierarchy of values associated with an expression looks like:

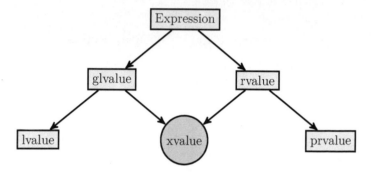

Figure 1.1: Expression Value Category Taxonomy

1. *lvalue* : This name came because earlier meaning was associated with its appearance in the left-hand side of an assignment.

   - An *lvalue* designates a function or an object.
   - If *ptr* is a pointer to an object or a function, then *ptr* is an *lvalue* expression.
   - The result of calling a function whose return type is an lvalue reference is an lvalue.

2. *xvalue* : It stands for an *expiring value*.

   - The result of calling a function whose return type is an *rvalue reference* is an xvalue.
   - It refers to an object, usually near the end of its lifetime, so that its resources may be moved.

3. *glvalue* : It stands for *generalized lvalue*. Thus it refers to either an lvalue or xvalue. glvalues can also have incomplete types.

4. *rvalue* : This name came because earlier meaning was associated with its appearance in the right-hand side of an assignment.

It is

- an xvalue

- a temporary object

- a subobject

- a value that is not associated with an object.

5. *prvalue* : It stands for *pure rvalue*, i.e., an rvalue that is not an xvalue.

- A prvalue holds the result of a function whose return type is not a reference.

- The value of a literal, like 10, true or 1.2e3 is a prvalue.

- Class prvalues can have cv-qualified types.

- non-class prvalues always have cv-unqualified types.

- prvalue is a complete type or a void type.

** Question 48   alignment

What is an *alignment*?

Solution of Question 48

An *alignment* is the number of bytes between successive addresses at which a given object can be allocated.

- Every alignment value is a non-negative integral power of two.

- It is represented as an integral constant of the type std::size_t.

- The alignment requirement of a complete type, an array or a reference to a complete object type can be found using an *alignof* expression.

- fundamental alignment $\leq$ alignof(std::max_align_t) $<$ extended alignment.

** Question 49   lvalue to rvalue conversion

What is Lvalue-to-rvalue conversion?

Solution of Question 49

Technically it is *glvalue* to *prvalue* conversion.

- For a complete type T, which is not a function or array can be converted to a *prvalue*.

- For incomplete type, the conversion has undefined behavior.

- For a class type T, *glvalue* should be either an object of type T or an object of a type derived from T.

- The object should be initialized.

- For a non-class type T, the type of the prvalue is without any const and/or volatile version of type T.

- For a class type T, the type of the prvalue is T.

- For a class type T, the conversion copy-initializes a temporary of type T from the glvalue and the result of the conversion is a prvalue for the temporary.

- *glvalue* of type *std::nullptr_t* then *prvalue* result is a null pointer constant.

* Question 50   non-const to const conversion

What is the output of the program ?

Program 1.43: non-const to const conversion

```
1 int  main ( )
2 {
3     const  char  c  =  ' c ' ;
4
5     char*  pc ;
6
7     const  char**  pcc  =  &pc ;
8
9       *pcc  =  &c ;
10
11      *pc  =  'C' ;
12 }
```

Solution of Question 50

This program doesn't get compiled. The compiler error is:

```
const.cpp:4:14:
error: cannot initialize a variable of type
 'const char **' with
        an rvalue of type 'char **'
const char** pcc = &pc;
             ^     ~~~

1 error generated
```

The reason for not allowing the conversion from non-const to const on the line number 7 is to safe-guard a program from inadvertently modifying a const object on line number 11.

** Question 51   xvalue rvalue

In the program, figure out *xvalue* and *lvalue*.

Program 1.44: xvalue rvalue

```
1 struct A
2 {
3     int i;
4 };
5
6 A&& operator+(A, A);
7
8 A&& f();
9
10 int main()
11 {
12     A a;
13
14     A&& a1 = static_cast<A&&>(a);
15 }
```

Solution of Question 51

The following expressions are *xvalues*:

- f()

- f().m

- static_cast<A&&>(a)

- $a + a$

The expression *ar* is an *lvalue*.

** Question 52 literal and lvalue

Is literal an *lvalue*?

Solution of Question 52

A string literal is an *lvalue*. All other literals are *prvalues*.

*** Question 53 valid usage of this pointer

Program 1.45: valid usage of this pointer

```cpp
1 class Outer
2 {
3     int a[sizeof(*this)];
4
5     unsigned int sz = sizeof(*this);
6
7     void f()
8     {
9         int b[sizeof(*this)];
10
11         struct Inner
12         {
13             int c[sizeof(*this)];
14         };
15     }
16 };
17
18 int main() {}
```

Solution of Question 53

This program doesn't get compiled. The compiler error is:

```
this.cpp:3:19:
error: invalid use of 'this' outside of a
non-static member
        function
    int a[sizeof(*this)];
                 ^
this.cpp:13:27:
error: invalid use of 'this' outside of a
```

```
non-static member
        function
            int c[sizeof(*this)];
                    ^
2 errors generated.
```

It is evident from this compiler error that usage of *this* is not valid on line numbers 3 and 13 because line number 3 is not inside a member function and line number 13 is not inside a member function of the class *Inner*.

** Question 54   sizeof

What is the output of the program ?

Program 1.46: sizeof

```cpp
1 #include <iostream>
2 #include <iomanip>
3
4 struct A
5 {
6     int i;
7 };
8
9 int main()
10 {
11     std::cout << sizeof(A::i) << std::endl;
12     std::cout << sizeof(A::i + 10) << std::endl;
13     std::cout << sizeof(A::i - 10) << std::endl;
14
15     std::cout << std::boolalpha;
16
17     std::cout << (sizeof(A::i + 20)
18                   ==
19                   sizeof(A::i - 20))
20                << std::endl;
21 }
```

Solution of Question 54

Output of the program is:

```
4
4
```

```
4
true
```

** Question 55   lambda and sorting

Write a function to sort a vector of floats based upon absolute values.

Solution of Question 55

We can use lambda expression to create simple unnamed function object:

Program 1.47: lambda and sorting

```cpp
1 #include <algorithm>
2 #include <cmath>
3 #include <vector>
4
5 void abssort(std::vector<float> vf)
6 {
7     std::sort(vf.begin(),
8               vf.end(),
9               [](float a, float b)
10              {
11                   return std::abs(a)
12                       <
13                       std::abs(b);
14              }
15              );
16 }
```

The evaluation of a lambda-expression results in a prvalue temporary known as *closure object*.

** Question 56   type of lambda

What is the type of a lambda expression ?

Solution of Question 56

The type of a lambda expression is a unique and unnamed class type except union type. It is also known as *closure type*. Please note that this class type is not an aggregate.

** Question 57   return type of lambda

How the return type of the following lambda expressions are determined?

Program 1.48: return type of lambda

```
1 auto  x1  =  [ ] ( int  i ) {  return  i ;  };
2 auto  x2  =  [ ] {  return  {  1,  2  };  };
```

Solution of Question 57

If the trailing return type of a lambda expression is missing then it is the type of the returned expression after

- lvalue-to-rvalue conversion

- array-to-pointer conversion

- function-to-pointer conversion

Otherwise it is void.

Hence the return type of the lambda expression on line number 1 is *int*. Because a braced initializer list is not an expression, hence {1, 2} is not an expression. This implies that the return type is *void* for the lambda expression on line 2. So this will result into compiler error.

*** **Question 58**   **lambda and default argument**

Which of the following lambda expressions are valid?

Program 1.49: lambda and default argument

```
1 void  func ( )
2 {
3      int  i  =  1;
4
5      void  g1 ( int  =  ( [ i ] {  return  i ;  } ) ( ) ) ;
6      void  g2 ( int  =  ( [ i ] {  return  0 ;  } ) ( ) ) ;
7      void  g3 ( int  =  ( [ = ] {  return  i ;  } ) ( ) ) ;
8      void  g4 ( int  =  ( [ − ] {  return  0 ;  } ) ( ) ) ;
9      void  g5 ( int  =  ( [ ] {  return  sizeof  i ;  } ) ( ) )
             ;
10 }
```

Solution of Question 58

A lambda-expression appearing in a default argument cannot not implicitly or explicitly capture any entity, hence the lambda expressions appearing on line numbers 5, 6 and 7 will raise compiler error:

```
lambda2.cpp:5:20:
error: lambda expression in default
argument cannot capture
        any entity
    void g1(int = ([i]{ return i; })());
                   ^

lambda2.cpp:6:20:
error: lambda expression in default
argument cannot capture
        any entity
    void g2(int = ([i]{ return 0; })());
                   ^

lambda2.cpp:7:20:
error: lambda expression in default
argument cannot capture
        any entity
    void g3(int = ([=]{ return i; })());
                   ^

3 errors generated.
```

****** Question 59   nested lambda expressions**

What is the output of the program ?

Program 1.50: nested lambda expressions

```cpp
#include <iostream>

int main()
{
    int a = 1, b = 1, c = 1;

    auto m1 = [a, &b, &c]() mutable
    {
        auto m2 = [a, b, &c]() mutable
        {
            std::cout << a << b << c
            << std::endl;

            a = 4; b = 4; c = 4;
        };

        a = 3; b = 3; c = 3;
```

```
19         m2 ( ) ;
20      } ;
21
22      a = 2;  b = 2;  c = 2;
23
24      m1 ( ) ;
25
26      std :: cout << a << b << c << std :: endl ;
27 }
```

Solution of Question 59

```
123
234
```

*** **Question 60   type of decltype((auto variable))**

What is the type of the expression *decltype((x))*, where x is an auto variable?

Solution of Question 60

Type of the expression *decltype((x))* is *const x &*, where x is an auto variable.

For example, in the following example:

Program 1.51: type of decltype((x))

```cpp
1 void  func ()
2 {
3      float  x,  &r = x;
4
5      [=]
6      {
7           decltype (x)  y1;
8
9           decltype ((x))  y2 = y1;
10
11          decltype (r)  r1 = y1;
12
13          decltype ((r))  r2 = y2;
14      };
15 }
```

the type of y1 is float, y2 is float const &, r1 is float & and r2 is float const &.

*** Question 61   brace initializer list as subscript

Can brace-init-list be used as a subscript ?

Solution of Question 61

It can not used as built-in subscript operator, but can be
used with user-define subscript operator where it will be treated
as the initializer for the subscript argument of the operator[] as
can be seen in this program:

Program 1.52: brace initializer list as subscript

```
1 #include <initializer_list >
2
3 struct A
4 {
5     int operator [] ( std :: initializer_list <int
         >);
6 };
7
8 int main ()
9 {
10    A a;
11
12    a[{1,2,3}] = 10;
13
14    int b[5];
15
16    b[{1, 2, 3}] = 20;
17 }
```

Here line 12 is ok, but line 16 is error.

** Question 62   Pseudo Destructor

What is a *pseudo destructor*?

Solution of Question 62

A *pseudo destructor* is a destructor of a nonclass type, which
will only be used as the operand for the function call operator
(), and the result of such a call has type *void*. The following
example calls the pseudo destructor for an integer type:

Program 1.53: Pseudo Destructor

```
1 #include <iostream>
2
3 typedef int Integer ;
4
5 int main ()
6 {
```

```
 7      Integer  i  =  100;
 8
 9      i . Integer :: ~ Integer ( ) ;
10
11      std :: cout  <<  "i ␣ : ␣"  <<  i  <<  std :: endl;
12
13      i  =  200;
14
15      std :: cout  <<  "i ␣ : ␣"  <<  i  <<  std :: endl;
16 }
```

The call to the pseudo destructor

```
i.Integer::~Integer()
```

has no effect at all.

Object i has not been destroyed; the assignment i = 200 is still valid.

Output of this program is:

```
i : 100
i : 200
```

Because pseudo destructors require the syntax for explicitly calling a destructor for a nonclass type to be valid, we can write code without having to know whether or not a destructor exists for a given type.

** Question 63   Dynamic Cast

What is *Dynamic Cast*?

Solution of Question 63

dynamic_cast<T>(v) is the result of converting the expression *v* to type *T*, where *T* is

- a pointer or reference to complete class type, or

- pointer to const/volatile void.

Please note that it doesn't cast away the constness.

1. If T is a pointer type, then v is a prvalue of a pointer to complete class type $\implies$ the result is a prvalue of type T.

2. If T is an lvalue reference type, then v is an lvalue of a complete class type $\implies$ the result is an lvalue of the type referred to by T.

3. If T is an rvalue reference type, then v is an expression having a complete class type $\implies$ the result is an xvalue of the type referred to by T.

4. If the type of v is the same as T, or it is the same as T except that the class object type in T is more cv-qualified than the class object type in v, the result is v (converted if necessary).

5. If the value of v is a null pointer value in the pointer case, the result is the null pointer value of type T.

** Question 64   Dynamic Cast vs Base/Derived

How *Dynamic Cast* operates in case of Base/Derived class scenarios?

Solution of Question 64

Let us assume that B is a base class of D.

- If T is a pointer type to B and v is pointer to D, then the result is a pointer to the unique subobject of the D object pointed to by v.

- if T is a reference to B and v is of type D, then the result is the unique B subobject of the D object referred to by v.

- If T is an lvalue reference then the result is an lvalue.

- If T is an rvalue reference then the result is an xvalue.

In the example below, dynamic cast is same as $B^*\ bp\ =\ dp;$:

Program 1.54: Dynamic Cast vs Base/Derived

```
1 struct B {};
2
3 struct D : B {};
4
5 void func(D* dp)
6 {
7     B* bp = dynamic_cast<B*>(dp);
8 }
```

*** Question 65   Dynamic Cast vs void

What is the result of *dynamic_cast<T>(v)* when *T* is a
pointer to void ?

Solution of Question 65

- The result is a pointer to the most derived object pointed
  to by v, or

- a run-time check is applied to see if the object pointed or
  referred to by v can be converted to the type pointed or
  referred to by T.

*** Question 66   Dynamic Cast Run-time Check

What is the result of *dynamic_cast<T>(v)* when *T* is a
pointer to a class *A* ?

Solution of Question 66

- If, in the most derived object pointed (referred) to by v,
  v points (refers) to a public base class subobject of a A
  object, and if only one object of type A is derived from
  the subobject pointed (referred) to by v the result points
  (refers) to that A object.

- Otherwise, if v points (refers) to a public base class subobject of the most derived object, and the type of the
  most derived object has a base class, of type A, that is
  unambiguous and public, the result points (refers) to the
  A subobject of the most derived object.

- Otherwise, the run-time check fails.

- The value of a failed cast to pointer type is the null pointer
  value of the required result type.

- A failed cast to reference type throws std::bad_cast.

*** Question 67   Understanding Dynamic Cast

what is the output of the program ?

Program 1.55: Understanding Dynamic Cast

```
1 #include <cassert>
2 #include <typeinfo>
3 #include <iostream>
4
5 class A
6 {
7     virtual void f() {}
8 };
9
10 class B
11 {
12     virtual void g() {}
13 };
14
15 class D : public virtual A, private B
16 {
17 };
18
19 void func()
20 {
21     D d;
22
23     B* bp = (B*)&d;
24
25     A* ap = &d;
26
27     try
28     {
29         D& dr = dynamic_cast<D&>(*bp);
30     }
31
32     catch(std::bad_cast & e)
33     {
34         std::cout << "Exception is : "
35             << e.what() << std::endl;
36     }
37
38     ap = dynamic_cast<A*>(bp);
39
40     assert(ap == nullptr);
41
42     bp = dynamic_cast<B*>(ap);
43
44     assert(ap == nullptr);
45
46     ap = dynamic_cast<A*>(&d);
47
48     assert(ap != nullptr);
49
```

```
50    //bp = dynamic_cast<B*>(&d);
51 }
52
53 int main()
54 {
55    func();
56 }
```

Solution of Question 67

Output of the program is

```
Exception is : std::bad_cast
```

- On line 23 : cast needed to break protection
- On line 25 : public derivation, no cast needed
- cast fails on line numbers 29, 38 and 42.
- line 50 will result into the compiler error

```
    dynamic_cast1.cpp:50:10:
    error: cannot cast 'D' to
    its private base class 'B'
    bp = dynamic_cast<B*>(&d);
         ^
dynamic_cast1.cpp:15:29:
note: declared private here
class D : public virtual A, private B
                                   ^~~~~~~~~
1 error generated.
```

*** **Question 68**   **Understanding Dynamic Cast**

Review the program:

Program 1.56: Understanding Dynamic Cast

```
1 #include <typeinfo>
2 #include <cassert>
3
```

```
 4 struct A
 5 {
 6     virtual void f() {}
 7 };
 8
 9 struct B
10 {
11     virtual void g() {}
12 };
13
14 struct D : virtual A, private B
15 {
16 };
17
18 struct E : D, B
19 {
20 };
21
22 struct F : E, D
23 {
24 };
25
26 void func()
27 {
28     F f;
29
30     A* ap = &f;
31
32     D* dp = dynamic_cast<D*>(ap);
33
34     assert(dp == nullptr);
35
36 //    E* ep = (E*)ap;
37
38     E* ep1 = dynamic_cast<E*>(ap);
39
40     assert(ep1 != nullptr);
41 }
42
43 int main()
44 {
45     func();
46 }
```

Solution of Question 68

- line 30 succeeds because it finds unique A.

- line 32 fails because f has two D subobjects

- line 36 results into compiler error because of cast from virtual base

```
dynamic_cast2.cpp:36:13:
error: cannot cast 'A *'
to 'E *' via virtual base 'A'
E* ep = (E*)ap;
        ^~~~~~
1 error generated.
```

** Question 69   typeid and const/volatile

Is const/volatile qualifier applicable to the result of *typeid* operator ?

Solution of Question 69

No, top level cv-qualifiers are simply ignored as is evident in the program below:

Program 1.57: typeid and const/volatile

```
1 #include <cassert>
2 #include <typeinfo>
3
4 struct A {};
5
6 int main()
7 {
8     A a1;
9
10    const A a2 = a1;
11
12    assert(typeid(a1) == typeid(a2));
13
14    assert(typeid(A)== typeid(const A));
15
16    assert(typeid(A) == typeid(a2));
17
18    assert(typeid(A) == typeid(const A&));
19
20    assert(typeid(A) == typeid(const volatile
          A));
21
22    assert(typeid(A) == typeid(volatile A&));
23 }
```

** Question 70   static cast

What is *static_cast<T>(v)* ?

Solution of Question 70

static_cast<T>(v) is the result of converting the expression v to type T.

- If T is an lvalue reference type or an rvalue reference to function type, the result is an lvalue

- if T is an rvalue reference to object type, the result is an xvalue

- otherwise, the result is a prvalue.

- The static_cast operator shall not cast away constness.

** Question 71   static cast and base/derived

Is the following program valid?

Program 1.58: static cast and base/derived

```
1 #include <cassert>
2 #include <typeinfo>
3
4 struct A {};
5
6 int main()
7 {
8     A a1;
9
10    const A a2   = a1;
11
12    assert(typeid(a1) == typeid(a2));
13
14    assert(typeid(A)== typeid(const A));
15
16    assert(typeid(A) == typeid(a2));
17
18    assert(typeid(A) == typeid(const A&));
19
20    assert(typeid(A) == typeid(const volatile
          A));
21
22    assert(typeid(A) == typeid(volatile A&));
23 }
```

Solution of Question 71

Yes because it produces lvalue to the original d object.

Let us assume that B is a base class of D.

B can be cast to a reference of D if a valid standard conversion from a pointer to D to a pointer to B exists provided:

- B is neither a virtual base class of D nor

- a base class of a virtual base class of D

If the object of type B is actually a subobject of an object of type D, the result refers to the enclosing object of type D as illustrated by this example.

** Question 72   static cast and inaccessible base

Can static cast be used with private base classes ?

Solution of Question 72

No. For example

Program 1.59: static cast and base/derived

```
 1 #include <cassert>
 2 #include <typeinfo>
 3
 4 struct A {};
 5
 6 int main()
 7 {
 8     A a1;
 9
10     const A a2 = a1;
11
12     assert(typeid(a1) == typeid(a2));
13
14     assert(typeid(A)== typeid(const A));
15
16     assert(typeid(A) == typeid(a2));
17
18     assert(typeid(A) == typeid(const A&));
19
20     assert(typeid(A) == typeid(const volatile
           A));
21
22     assert(typeid(A) == typeid(volatile A&));
23 }
```

This program doesn't get compiled. The error is:

```
static_cast2.cpp:7:5: error: cannot cast
private base class 'B' to 'D'
    static_cast<D*>((B*)0);
    ^

static_cast2.cpp:3:12: note: declared private here
struct D : private B { };
              ^~~~~~~~~

static_cast2.cpp:9:5: error: cannot cast 'D' to its
private base class 'B'
    static_cast<int B::*>((int D::*)0);
    ^

static_cast2.cpp:3:12: note: declared private here
struct D : private B { };
              ^~~~~~~~~
```

*** Question 73   static cast and const cast

Can static cast be used to add the constness?

Solution of Question 73

Yes.

1. cast A * to void *

2. cast the above result void * to const A *

Program 1.60: static cast and base/derived

```
1 #include <cassert>
2
3 struct A {};
4
5 int main()
6 {
7     A* aptr1 = new A;
8
9     const A* aptr2 =
10         static_cast<const A*>(
11             static_cast<void*>(aptr1)
12         );
13
14     assert(aptr1 == aptr2);
15 }
```

**** Question 74   static cast to and fro

Is the following program valid?

Program 1.61: static cast to and fro

```
 1 #include <cassert>
 2
 3 struct A {};
 4
 5 struct B {};
 6
 7 int main()
 8 {
 9     A* aptr = new A;
10
11     A * aptr1 =
12         static_cast<A*>(
13             static_cast<void*>(
14                 static_cast<B*>(
15                     static_cast<void*>(aptr)
16                 )
17             )
18         );
19
20     assert(aptr == aptr1);
21 }
```

Solution of Question 74

Yes.

1. cast A * to void *

2. cast the above result void * to B *

3. cast the above result B * to void *

4. cast the above result void * back to the original pointer A *

* Question 75   type of base class member

What is the type of *&B::i* ?

Program 1.62: type of base class member

```
 1 struct A
 2 {
 3     int i;
 4 };
 5
 6 struct B : A {};
```

Solution of Question 75

*int A::i *.*

**** Question 76   counting types

Write a program to count the number of types participating in a class template argument ?

Solution of Question 76

sizeof... operator yields the number of arguments provided for the parameter pack identifier.

Program 1.63: counting types

```cpp
#include <iostream>

template<class ... Types>
struct count_types
{
    static const std::size_t value
        =
    sizeof ... ( Types);
};

int main()
{
    std::cout << count_types<int, float >::
        value
            << std::endl;

    std::cout << count_types<int, float,
                            std::string >::
                            value
            << std::endl;

    std::cout << count_types<int >::value
            << std::endl;
}
```

Output of this program is

```
2
3
1
```

The result of sizeof and sizeof... is a constant of type std::size_t.

* Question 77   auto type specifier

What are the allocated types in the expressions below and what is the type of the variable x ?

```
new auto(1);
auto x = new auto('a');
```

Solution of Question 77

In the very first expression, the allocated type is int.
In the second expression, the allocated type is char.
Type of the variable x is *char* *.

* Question 78   type of new

What are the types of the following new expressions ?

1. new int

2. new int[20]

3. new int[i][20]

Solution of Question 78

1. type of new int is int *

2. type of new int[20] is int *

3. type of new int[i][20] is int (*)[20]

* Question 79   using new

Write an expression to create an array consisting of 20 pointers to function which takes no argument and returns an int.

Solution of Question 79

new (int (*[20])());

** Question 80   operator new

Explain the following expressions with respect to the operator new[](std::size_t, void*):

1. new T

2. new(10, ptr) T

3. new T[20]

4. new(2, ptr) T[5]

Solution of Question 80

1. new T results in a call of operator new(sizeof(T)),

2. new(10, ptr) T results in a call of operator new(sizeof(T), 10, ptr),

3. new T[20] results in a call of operator new[](sizeof(T)*20 + x)

4. new(10, ptr) T[50] results in a call of operator new[](sizeof(T)*50 + y, 10, f).

Here, x and y are non-negative unspecified values representing array allocation overhead; the result of the new-expression will be offset by this amount from the value returned by operator new[].

**** Question 81   placement operator

What is the problem with the following program?

Program 1.64: placement operator

```
1 #include <cstddef>
2
3 struct A
4 {
5     // Placement allocation function:
6     static void* operator new(
7                     std::size_t, std::size_t);
8
9     // non-placement deallocation function:
10    static void operator delete(
11                    void*, std::size_t);
12 };
13
14 int main()
15 {
16     A* ptr = new (0) A;
17 }
```

Solution of Question 81

A declaration of a placement deallocation function matches the declaration of a placement allocation function if it has the same number of parameters and, after parameter transformations, all parameter types except the first are identical. Any non-placement deallocation function matches a non-placement allocation function.

Hence this program is ll-formed: non-placement deallocation function matches placement allocation function thus resulting into the compiler error

```
custom_allocate.cpp:16:14:
error: 'new' expression with
placement arguments
        refers to non-placement 'operator delete'
    A* ptr = new (0) A;
             ^      ~
custom_allocate.cpp:10:17: note: 'operator delete'
declared here
        static void operator delete(
                    ^

1 error generated.
```

*** Question 82   illegal casting

What is the problem with the following program?

Program 1.65: illegal casting

```
1 struct A {};
2
3 struct B : A {};
4
5 struct C : A {};
6
7 struct D : B, C {};
8
9 A * func(D * ptr)
10 {
11     return (A*)(ptr);
12 }
```

Solution of Question 82

This results into the compiler error

```
cast.cpp:12:16: error: ambiguous conversion from
derived class 'D' to base
     class 'A':
  struct D -> struct B -> struct A
  struct D -> struct C -> struct A
  return (A*)(ptr);
               ^~~~~
1 error generated.
```

This is self-explanatory from this error description.

** Question 83   mutable and const

Is it possible to use a pointer to member that refers to a mutable member to modify a const class object?

Solution of Question 83

No.

For example, in the following program, pm refers to mutable member A::i which is being used to attempt modify the const object ca.

Program 1.66: mutable and const

```
1 struct A {};
2
3 struct B : A {};
4
5 struct C : A {};
6
7 struct D : B, C {};
8
9 A * func(D * ptr)
10 {
11     return (A*)(ptr);
12 }
```

** Question 84   pointer to member function

Write an expression to call the member function denoted by a pointer ptr_to_mfct for the object pointed to by ptr_to_obj where the member function takes an integer value 100 and returns nothing.

Solution of Question 84

```
(ptr_to_obj->*ptr_to_mfct)(100);
```

*** Question 85   relational operator and void *

Can a void * be compared to a const int * ?

Can int ** be compared to int *const * ?

Solution of Question 85

Yes for both.

For example, in the program below, on line number 11 : both converted to const void* before comparison and on line number 13 : Both converted to const int *const * before comparison.

Program 1.67: relational operator and void *

```
1  int  main()
2  {
3      void  *p;
4
5      const  int  *q;
6
7      int  **pi;
8
9      const  int  *const  *pci;
10
11     p <= q;
12
13     pi <= pci;
14 }
```

** Question 86   Pointers Comparison

What is the result of comparing two pointers p and q when

1. both point to the same object or function

2. both point one past the end of the same array

3. both are null

4. both point to object of type std::nullptr_t

5. both are void

Solution of Question 86

1.   • p<=q is true
     • p>=q is true
     • p < q is false
     • p > q is false

2.   • p<=q is true
     • p>=q is true
     • p < q is false
     • p > q is false

3.   • p<=q is true
     • p>=q is true
     • p < q is false
     • p > q is false

4.   • p<=q is true
     • p>=q is true
     • p < q is false
     • p > q is false

5. If both pointers represent the same address or are both the null pointer value, the result is true if the operator is <= or >= and false otherwise; otherwise the result is unspecified.

*** Question 87   Pointers to Members Comparison

What is the output of the program ?

Program 1.68: Pointers to Members Comparison

```cpp
#include <iostream>
#include <iomanip>

struct Base
{
    void func() {}
};
```

```
 8
 9 struct Derived1 : Base { };
10
11 struct Derived2 : Base { };
12
13 struct D : Derived1 , Derived2 { };
14
15 int main ()
16 {
17      std :: cout << std :: boolalpha ;
18
19      void (Base :: * pb) () = &Base :: func ;
20
21      void (Derived1 :: * pl) () = pb ;
22
23      std :: cout << "(pb == pl) : "
24                  << (pb == pl) << std :: endl ;
25
26      void (Derived2 :: * pr) () = pb ;
27
28      std :: cout << "(pb == pr) : "
29                  << (pb == pr) << std :: endl ;
30
31      void (D:: * pdl) () = pl ;
32
33      std :: cout << "(pdl == pl) : "
34                  << (pdl == pl) << std :: endl ;
35
36      void (D:: * pdr) () = pr ;
37
38      std :: cout << "(pdr == pr) : "
39                  << (pdr == pr) << std :: endl ;
40
41      std :: cout << "(pdr == pl) : "
42                  << (pdr == pr) << std :: endl ;
43
44      std :: cout << "(pdl == pr) : "
45                  << (pdl == pr) << std :: endl ;
46
47      std :: cout << "(pdl == pdr) : "
48                  << (pdl == pdr) << std :: endl ;
49 }
```

Solution of Question 87

```
(pb == pl) : true
(pb == pr) : true
(pdl == pl) : true
```

```
(pdr == pr) : true
(pdr == pl) : true
(pdl == pr) : false
(pdl == pdr) : false
```

* **Question 88**   brace initializer list and assignment

Review the program ?

Program 1.69: brace initializer list and assignment

```
 1 #include <complex>
 2
 3 int main ()
 4 {
 5     std :: complex<double> z ;
 6
 7     z = { 1, 2 };
 8
 9
10     int a, b;
11
12     a = b = { 1 };
13
14     a = { 1 } = b;
15 }
```

Solution of Question 88

Line number 7 means calling z.operator=({1,2})

Line number 12 means a = b = 1;

Line number 14 will raise a compiler error:

```
complex.cpp:14:15:
error: initializer list cannot be used
on the left hand side
      of operator '='
    a = { 1 } = b;
      ~~~~~ ^
1 error generated.
```

** **Question 89**   comma operator and argument

Will the following program compile? If yes, what is the output ?

Program 1.70: comma operator and argument

```
1 #include <iostream>
2
3 void func(int i)
4 {
5     std::cout << "i : " << i << std::endl;
6 }
7
8 int main()
9 {
10    int first, second;
11
12    func((first = 100, second = 200, first +
          second));
13 }
```

Solution of Question 89

Yes, the program compiles and the output is:

```
i : 300
```

*** Question 90   constexpr constructor

Will the following program compile?

How about if the line 20 is commented out ?

Program 1.71: constexpr constructor

```
1 int k = 100;
2
3 struct A
4 {
5     constexpr A(bool b)
6     :
7     m( b ? 10 : k)
8     {
9     }
10
11    int m;
12 };
13
14 int main()
15 {
16    constexpr int i = A(true).m;
17
18    static_assert(i == 10, "");
```

```
19
20      //constexpr  int  j  =  A(false).m;
21 }
```

Solution of Question 90

Yes, the program compiles.

If the line 20 is commented out, it results into the compiler error:

```
constexpr_constructor.cpp:20:19:
error: constexpr variable 'j' must be
        initialized by a constant expression
    constexpr int j = A(false).m;
              ^         ~~~~~~~~~~
constexpr_constructor.cpp:7:17:
note: read of non-const variable 'k' is not
        allowed in a constant expression
    m( b ? 10 : k)
              ^
constexpr_constructor.cpp:20:23:
note: in call to 'A(false)'
    constexpr int j = A(false).m;
                      ^
constexpr_constructor.cpp:1:5: note: declared here
int k = 100;
    ^

1 error generated.
```

This is because the value of 'k' is not usable in a constant expression, since 'int k' is not a const.

** Question 91   translation vs runtime

What is the output of the program ?

Is it reliable enough ?

Program 1.72: translation vs runtime
```
1 #include <iostream>
2
3 void func ()
4 {
5       char arr [1 + int (1 + 0.3 − 0.6 − 0.6)];
```

```
6
7    int  size = 1 + int(1 + 0.3 − 0.6 − 0.6);
8
9    std::cout << std::boolalpha;
10
11   std::cout << (sizeof(arr) == size)
12             << std::endl;
13 }
14
15 int  main()
16 {
17     func();
18 }
```

Solution of Question 91

It prints *true*, but it is not reliable because the expression on line 5 must be evaluated during translation, but the expression on line 7 may be evaluated at runtime.

Hence it is unspecified whether the value of f() will be true or false.

**** Question 92   literal class and integral constant

Will is the output of the program?

Will the program compile after commenting out the line number 35 ?

Program 1.73: literal class and integral constant

```
1 #include <iostream>
2
3 struct A
4 {
5     constexpr A(int i)  : m(i)  { }
6
7     constexpr operator int()
8     {
9         return m + 100;
10    }
11
12    constexpr operator long()
13    {
14        return m + 200;
15    }
16
17 private:
18     int m;
19 };
```

```
20
21 template<int n>
22 struct B
23 {
24      enum  {  RET  =  n  };
25 };
26
27 int  main ()
28 {
29      constexpr A  a  =  10;
30
31      B<a>  b;
32
33      std :: cout  <<  (B<a >::RET)  <<  std :: endl;
34
35      //int  array [a];
36 }
```

Solution of Question 92

It will print *110*.

If an expression of literal class type is used in a context where an integral constant expression is required, then that class type should have a single non-explicit conversion function to an integral or enumeration type and that conversion function should be constexpr.

Hence after commenting out the line number 35, it will raise a compiler error because of ambiguous conversion:

```
literal_class.cpp: In function 'int main()':
literal_class.cpp:35:16:
 error: ambiguous default type
conversion from 'const A'
     int array[a];
                ^
literal_class.cpp:35:16:
error:   candidate conversions
include 'constexpr A::operator int() const' and
'constexpr A::operator long int() const'
```

* Question 93   scope of conditional variable

Will is the scope of a conditional variable?

Will the program compile ?

Program 1.74: scope of conditional variable

```
1  int  main ()
2  {
3      if (int  first  =  10)
4      {
5          int  first ;
6      }
7      else
8      {
9          int  first ;
10     }
11 }
```

Solution of Question 93

A name introduced by a declaration in a condition is in scope from its point of declaration until the end of the substatements controlled by the condition.

Hence the program will not compile due to redeclarations of integer i.

```
scope_conditional_variable.cpp:
In function 'int main()':
scope_conditional_variable.cpp:5:13: error:
redeclaration of 'int first'
         int first;
             ^
scope_conditional_variable.cpp:3:12: error:
'int first' previously declared here
     if(int first = 10)
            ^
scope_conditional_variable.cpp:9:13: error:
redeclaration of 'int first'
         int first;
             ^
scope_conditional_variable.cpp:3:12: error:
'int first' previously declared here
     if(int first = 10)
            ^
```

** Question 94   scope of conditional variable

Will is the output of the program ?

Program 1.75: scope of conditional variable

```cpp
#include <iostream>

struct A
{
    int m;

    A(int i) : m(i)
    {
        std::cout << "A("
            << m << ")" << std::endl;
    }

    ~A()
    {
        std::cout << "~A()" << std::endl;
    }

    operator bool()
    {
        return m != 0;
    }
};

void func()
{
    int i = 10;

    while(A a = i)
    {
        i = 0;
    }
}



int main()
{
    func();
}
```

Solution of Question 94

Output of the program is:

```
A(10)
```

```
~A()
A(0)
~A()
```

The variable created in a condition is destroyed and created with each iteration of the loop.

In the while-loop, the constructor and destructor are each called twice, once for the condition that succeeds and once for the condition that fails.

*** Question 95   simulation of while loop

Simulate the while loop of the previous program.

Solution of Question 95

Program 1.76: simulation of while loop

```cpp
#include <iostream>

struct A
{
    int m;

    A(int i) : m(i)
    {
        std::cout << "A("
                  << m << ")" << std::endl;
    }

    ~A()
    {
        std::cout << "~A()" << std::endl;
    }

    operator bool()
    {
        return m != 0;
    }
};

void func_simulate()
{
    int i = 10;

    label:
    {
        A a = i;
```

```
32          if ( a )
33          {
34              i = 0;
35              goto label;
36          }
37       }
38 }
39
40
41 int main ()
42 {
43      func_simulate ();
44 }
```

* Question 96   range for loop

Given an integer array like the following, write a program
to print its contents using range for loop:

```
int array[5] = { 1, 2, 3, 4, 5 };
```

Solution of Question 96

```
for (int& x : array)
std::cout << x << std::endl;
```

*** Question 97   simulation of range for loop

Simulate range for loop using simple for loop statement.
There are two kinds of range for statements:

1. for (for-range-declaration : expression) statement

2. for (for-range-declaration : braced-init-list) statement

Solution of Question 97

Both of these can be simulated like the following:

```
{
      auto && range = range-init;

      for ( auto begin = std::begin(range),
                  end = std::end(range);
            begin != end; ++begin )
      {
            for-range-declaration = *begin;
            statement
      }
}
```

* Question 98   return brace-init-list

Is the following program valid ?

Program 1.77: return brace-init-list

```
1 #include <utility>
2 #include <string>
3
4 std::pair<std::string, int>
5 func(const char* p, int x)
6 {
7       return {p, x};
8 }
```

Solution of Question 98

Yes.

A return statement with a braced-init-list initializes the object or reference to be returned from the function by copy-list-initialization from the specified initializer list.

* Question 99   attributes

Is the following program valid ?

Program 1.78: specifying attributes

```
1 [[noreturn, nothrow]] void f [[noreturn]] ();
```

Solution of Question 99

Yes.

** Question 100   typedef and const

In the program below, what is pointer_to_char?

- char* const, or

- const char*

```
typedef char*  pointer_to_char;
void func(const pointer_to_char);
```

Solution of Question 100

pointer_to_char is char* const.

** Question 101   storage class specifiers

How many types of storage class specifiers are available ?
Solution of Question 101

Storage class specifiers are:

1. register

2. static

3. thread_local

4. extern

5. mutable

*** Question 102   inline function

What is an inline function?
Solution of Question 102

- A function declaration with an inline specifier declares an inline function

- The inline specifier indicates to the implementation that inline substitution of the function body at the point of call is to be preferred to the usual function call mechanism. An implementation is not required to perform this inline substitution at the point of call.

- A function defined within a class definition is an inline function. The inline specifier may not appear on a block scope function declaration.

- If the inline specifier is used in a friend declaration, that declaration will be a definition or the function has previously been declared inline.

- An inline function is defined in every translation unit in which it is odr-used and has exactly the same definition in every case.

- If a function with external linkage is declared inline in one translation unit, it is declared inline in all translation units in which it appears.

- An inline function with external linkage shall have the same address in all translation units.

- A static local variable in an extern inline function always refers to the same object.

- A string literal in the body of an extern inline function is the same object in different translation units.

- A type defined within the body of an extern inline function is the same type in every translation unit.

Chapter 2

Constant Expression

*** Question 103 basics of constexpr

Can *constexpr* be applied to

1. a class declaration

2. a class definition

3. the definition of an object

4. the declaration of a function

5. the definition of a function

6. function parameters

7. the declaration of a function template

8. the definition of a function template

9. the declaration of a static data member of a literal type

Solution of Question 103

1. No

 The following is an error because A is declaration of the type A.

```
constexpr struct A;
```

2. No

The following is an error because A is definition of the type A.

```
constexpr struct A {};
```

3. Yes

```
constexpr A a;
constexpr int i = 10;
```

4. Yes

```
constexpr void func();
struct A
{
    constexpr void g();
};
```

5. Yes

```
constexpr void func() {}
```

6. No

The following is an error because constexpr is applied to the integer parameter i of the function *func*

```
void func(constexpr int i) {}
```

7. Yes

8. Yes

9. Yes

*** Question 104   basics of constexpr

Can *constexpr* be applied to the following ?

1.
```
extern constexpr int i;
```

2.
```
constexpr void f();

struct A
{
    A() { f(); }
};

constexpr A a;
```

Solution of Question 104

1. No, because it is not a definition.

2. Declaration of the function f is fine in *constexpr void f();*, but definition of the variable a is not fine because the definition of f is not available yet.

*** Question 105   basics of constexpr

Which of the following is true?

1. If any declaration of a function or function template has constexpr specifier, then all its declarations should contain the constexpr specifier.

2. An explicit specialization cannot differ from the template declaration with respect to the constexpr specifier.

Solution of Question 105

1. True.

2. False.

*** Question 106   constexpr function

What is *constexpr function* ?

Solution of Question 106

A constexpr specifier used in the declaration of a function that is not a constructor declares that function to be a constexpr function.

- constexpr function is implicitly inline.

- it cannot be virtual

- its return type is a literal type or a reference to literal type

- each of its parameter types is a literal type or a reference to literal type

- its function-body is

```
{ return constant-expression ; }
```

*** Question 107   usage of constexpr function

Which of the following is a valid *constexpr function* ?

1.
```
constexpr int square(int x)
{
    return x * x;
}
```

```
     constexpr long long_max()
2.   {
         return 2147483647;
     }
```

```
     constexpr int abs(int x)
3.   {
         return x < 0 ? -x : x;
     }
```

```
4.   constexpr void f(int x) {}
```

```
     constexpr int prev(int x)
5.   {
         return --x;
     }
```

```
     constexpr int func(int x)
6.   {
         int y = x;
         return y;
     }
```

Solution of Question 107

1. Ok

2. Ok

3. Ok

4. Error because return type is void.

5. Error because of decrement operation

6. Error because the body doesn't contain just return expression.

*** Question 108   constexpr constructor

What is *constexpr constructor* ?

Solution of Question 108

A constexpr specifier used in a constructor declaration declares that constructor to be a constexpr constructor.

- constexpr constructor is implicitly inline.

- each of its parameter types is a literal type or a reference to literal type.

- its function-body is not a function-try-block.

- its function-body is empty, i.e., there is no statement in its function-body.

- every non-static data member and base class sub-object is initialized.

- every constructor involved in initializing non-static data members and base class sub-objects is a constexpr constructor

- every assignment-expression that is an initializer-clause appearing directly or indirectly within a brace-or-equal-initializer for a non-static data member that is not named by a mem-initializer-id is a constant expression.

- every implicit conversion used in converting a constructor argument to the corresponding parameter type and converting a full-expression to the corresponding member type is a constant expression.

```
struct A
{
    explicit constexpr A(int i = 0)
        :
    m(i)
    {
    }

private:
    int m;
};
```

A trivial copy/move constructor is also a constexpr constructor.

*** Question 109   constexpr function example

What is the output of the program ?

Program 2.1: constexpr function example

```
1 #include <iostream>
2
3 constexpr int func(void *)
4 {
5     return 10;
6 }
7
8 constexpr int func (...)
9 {
10    return 20;
11 }
12
13 constexpr int invoke1_func ()
14 {
15    return func(0);
16 }
17
18 constexpr int invoke2_func(int n)
19 {
20    return func(n);
21 }
22
23 constexpr int invoke3_func(int n)
24 {
25    return func(n * 0);
26 }
27
```

```
28 int main ()
29 {
30     std :: cout << "invoke1_func () : "
31         << invoke1_func () << std :: endl;
32
33     std :: cout << "invoke2_func (200) : "
34         << invoke2_func (200) << std :: endl;
35
36     std :: cout << "invoke2_func (0) : "
37         << invoke2_func (0) << std :: endl;
38
39     std :: cout << "invoke3_func (200) : "
40         << invoke3_func (200) << std :: endl;
41 }
```

Solution of Question 109

Output of the program is:

```
invoke1_func() : 10
invoke2_func(200) : 20
invoke2_func(0) : 20
invoke3_func(200) : 20
```

Please note that *invoke2_func* invokes *func(...)* even for n = 0.

** Question 110   constexpr function and substitution

What is the output of the program ?

Program 2.2: constexpr function and substitution

```
1 #include <iostream>
2
3 namespace A
4 {
5     constexpr int x = 10;
6
7     constexpr int func ()
8     {
9         return x;
10     }
11 } // namespace A
12
13 constexpr int x = 20;
14
15 constexpr int invoke_func ()
16 {
```

```
17        return A::func();
18  }
19
20  int main()
21  {
22        std::cout << "invoke_func() : "
23           << invoke_func() << std::endl;
24  }
```

Solution of Question 110

Output of the program is:

```
invoke_func() : 10
```

Please note that x is not looked up again after the substitution.

* Question 111   revise constexpr function

What is the output of the program ?

Program 2.3: revise constexpr function

```
1  #include <iostream>
2
3  constexpr int func(bool b)
4  {
5        return b ? throw 0 : 0;
6  }
7
8  constexpr int func()
9  {
10       throw 0;
11  }
12
13  int main()
14  {
15       func(true);
16  }
```

Solution of Question 111

This program doesn't get compiled. Compiler error is

```
constexpr_function1.cpp:10:5:
error: statement not allowed
```

```
in constexpr function
    throw 0;
    ^

1 error generated.
```

Another compiler gives the following error:

```
constexpr_function1.cpp:
In function 'constexpr int func()':
constexpr_function1.cpp:11:1:
error: body of constexpr
function 'constexpr int func()'
not a return-statement
    }
    ^
```

It is self-explanatory from the error-description.

** Question 112   revise constexpr constructor

Review the program.

Program 2.4: revise constexpr constructor

```
1 struct Base
2 {
3     constexpr Base(int i)
4     : m(0)
5     {}
6
7     int m;
8 };
9
10 int x;
11
12 struct Derived : Base
13 {
14     constexpr Derived()
15     :
16     Base(x)
17     {}
18 };
```

Solution of Question 112

This program doesn't get compiled. Compiler error is

```
constexpr_constructor1.cpp:14:15:
error: constexpr constructor never produces a
      constant expression [-Winvalid-constexpr]
      constexpr Derived()
              ^

constexpr_constructor1.cpp:16:10:
note: read of non-const variable 'x' is not
      allowed in a constant expression
      Base(x)
         ^

constexpr_constructor1.cpp:10:5:
note: declared here
      int x;
        ^

1 error generated.
```

Another compiler gives the following error:

```
constexpr_constructor1.cpp:
  In constructor 'constexpr Derived::Derived()':
constexpr_constructor1.cpp:17:6:
error: the value of 'x' is not usable
in a constant expression
      {}
       ^

constexpr_constructor1.cpp:10:5:
note: 'int x' is not const
  int x;
      ^
```

It is self-explanatory from the error-description.

*** Question 113   literal type

What is a *literal type* ?

Solution of Question 113

A type is a literal type if it is:

- a scalar type; or

- a class type with

  - a trivial copy constructor,
  - no non-trivial move constructor,
  - a trivial destructor,
  - a trivial default constructor or at least one constexpr constructor other than the copy or move constructor, and
  - all non-static data members and base classes of literal types; or

- an array of literal type.

*** Question 114   constexpr and literal type

What is problem with this program ?

Program 2.5: constexpr and literal type

```
1 struct A
2 {
3     A();
4
5     constexpr void func();
6 };
```

Solution of Question 114

This code doesn't get compiled. Compiler error is

```
constexpr_literal_type.cpp:5:20:
error: non-literal type 'A' cannot have
      constexpr members
    constexpr void func();
                   ^
constexpr_literal_type.cpp:1:8:
note: 'A' is not literal because it is not an
      aggregate and has no constexpr constructors
      other than copy or move
      constructors
struct A
       ^

1 error generated.
```

Another compiler gives the error below:

```
constexpr_literal_type.cpp:5:20:
error: enclosing class of constexpr non-static
member function 'void A::func() const' is not a
literal type
      constexpr void func();
                    ^
constexpr_literal_type.cpp:1:8: note:
'A' is not literal
because:
 struct A
        ^
constexpr_literal_type.cpp:1:8:
note:   'A' is not an aggregate, does not have a
trivial default constructor, and has
no constexpr constructor that is not a copy or move
constructor
```

It is self-explanatory from the error-description.

*** Question 115   constexpr and constructor

What is problem with this program ?

Program 2.6: constexpr and constructor
```
1 struct Point
2 {
3    int x, y;
4 };
5
6 constexpr Point p1 = { 10, 20 };
7
8 constexpr Point p2;
```

Solution of Question 115

This code doesn't get compiled. Compiler error is

```
constexpr_object.cpp:8:17:
error: default initialization of
an object of const
```

```
                    type 'const Point' requires a user-provided
                    default
                    constructor
            constexpr Point p2;
                         ^

            1 error generated.
```

Another compiler gives the error below:

```
constexpr_object.cpp:8:17:
error: uninitialized const 'p2'
[-fpermissive]
 constexpr Point p2;
                 ^

constexpr_object.cpp:1:8:
note: 'const struct Point' has no
user-provided default constructor
 struct Point
        ^

constexpr_object.cpp:3:9:
note: and the implicitly-defined
constructor does not initialize 'int Point::x'
     int x, y;
         ^
```

Please note that a constexpr specifier used in an object declaration declares the object as const which should be initialized and have literal type. If it is initialized by a constructor call, that call should be a constant expression, otherwise, every full-expression that appears in its initializer has to be a constant expression.

Chapter 3

Type Specifier

What is problem with this program ?

Program 3.1: const/volatile qualifier

```
1 struct X
2 {
3     mutable int i;
4     int j;
5 };
6
7 struct Y
8 {
9     X x;
10    Y();
11 };
12
13
14 int main()
15 {
16    const Y y;
17
18    y.x.i++;
19    y.x.j++;
20
21    Y* p = const_cast<Y*>(&y);
22    p->x.i = 99;
23    p->x.j = 99;
24
25
26    const int ci = 10;
27    ci = 11;
28
```

```
29    int  i = 20;
30    const int* cip ;
31    cip = &i ;
32    *cip = 4;
33
34    int* ip ;
35    ip = const_cast<int*>(cip) ;
36    *ip = 4;
37
38    const int* ciq = new const int (3) ;
39    int* iq = const_cast<int*>(ciq) ;
40    *iq = 4;
41 }
```

Solution of Question 116

This code doesn't get compiled. Compiler error is

```
const_volatile.cpp:19:10:
error: read-only variable is not assignable
    y.x.j++;
    ~~~~~^
const_volatile.cpp:27:8:
error: read-only variable is not assignable
    ci = 11;
    ~~  ^
const_volatile.cpp:32:10:
error: read-only variable is not assignable
    *cip = 4;
    ~~~~ ^
3 errors generated.
```

Another compiler gives the error below:

```
const_volatile.cpp: In function 'int main()':
const_volatile.cpp:19:10:
error: increment of member 'X::j' in
read-only object
    y.x.j++;
        ^
const_volatile.cpp:27:8:
error: assignment of read-only variable 'ci'
```

```
        ci = 11;
           ^

const_volatile.cpp:32:10:
error: assignment of read-only location '* cip'
        *cip = 4;
           ^
```

Please note that volatile is a hint to the implementation to avoid aggressive optimization involving the object because the value of the object might be changed by means undetectable by an implementation.

*** Question 117   decltype

What is the type of *decltype(expression)* in the program below ?

What is the output of the program ?

Program 3.2: decltype

```cpp
1 #include <iostream>
2
3 const int&& func ();
4
5 int i;
6
7 struct A
8 {
9     double d;
10 };
11
12 int main ()
13 {
14     const A* a = new A();
15
16     decltype(func()) e1 = i;
17
18     decltype(i) e2;
19
20     e2 = 5;
21
22     decltype(a->d) e3;
23
24     e3 = 10;
25
26     decltype((a->d)) e4 = e3;
27
28     e4 = 20;
29
```

```
30      std :: cout << e2 << e3 << e4 << std :: endl;
31 }
```

Solution of Question 117

This code doesn't get compiled. Compiler error is

```
decltype1.cpp:16:22:
error: rvalue reference to type
'const int' cannot bind to
    lvalue of type 'int'
    decltype(func()) e1 = i;
               ^    ~
decltype1.cpp:28:8: error: read-only variable is
not assignable
    e4 = 20;
    ~~ ^
2 errors generated.
```

Another compiler gives the error below:

```
decltype1.cpp: In function 'int main()':
decltype1.cpp:16:27:
error: cannot bind 'int' lvalue to
'const int&&'
    decltype(func()) e1 = i;
                ^
decltype1.cpp:28:8: error: assignment of read-only
reference 'e4'
    e4 = 20;
    ^
```

Type of the *decltype(expression)* are as follows:

- line 16 : type is *const int &&*

- line 19 : type is *int*

- line 26 : type is *double*

- line 26 : type is *const double &&*

*** Question 118   friend template parameter

How to declare a class template parameter as a friend of the class ?

Solution of Question 118

Let us try as the following:

Program 3.3: friend template parameter

```
1 template  <typename T>
2 struct  A
3 {
4       friend  class  T;
5 };
```

This code doesn't get compiled. Compiler error is

```
elaborated_type.cpp:4:18:
error: declaration of 'T' shadows
template parameter
    friend class T;
                 ^
elaborated_type.cpp:1:20:
note: template parameter is
declared here
template <typename T>
                   ^

1 error generated.
```

Another compiler gives the error below:

```
elaborated_type.cpp:4:18:
error: using template type
parameter 'T' after 'class'
    friend class T;
                 ^
elaborated_type.cpp:4:5:
error: friend declaration does not
name a class or function
    friend class T;
    ^
```

Instead, the following code is the correct one :

Program 3.4: friend template parameter

```
1 template <typename T>
2 struct A
3 {
4     friend T;
5 };
```

** Question 119   auto type specifier

What is the type of the following variables ?

Program 3.5: auto type specifier

```
1 auto x = 10;
2 const auto *v = &x, u = 20;
3 static auto y = 30.0;
4 auto int r;
```

Solution of Question 119

This code doesn't get compiled. Compiler error is

```
auto1.cpp:4:1:
warning: 'auto' storage class specifier
is not permitted in
        C++11, and will not be supported in future
        releases
        [-Wauto-storage-class]
auto int r;
^~~~~
auto1.cpp:4:10: error: illegal storage class on
file-scoped variable
auto int r;
         ^

1 warning and 1 error generated.
```

Another compiler gives the error below:

```
auto1.cpp:4:10: error: two or more data types in
declaration of 'r'
  auto int r;
           ^
```

The type of

- x is int

- v is const int*

- u is const int

- y is double

Please note that auto is not a storage-class-specifier, hence the error on the line 4.

*** **Question 120**   **auto vs template argument deduction**

What is the type of the variables a and b ?

Program 3.6: auto type specifier vs template argument deduction

```
1 #include <initializer_list>
2
3 auto a = { 1, 2 };
4 auto b = { 1, 2.0 };
```

Solution of Question 120

This code doesn't get compiled. Compiler error is

```
auto2.cpp:4:6: error: cannot deduce actual type
for variable 'b' with type
      'auto' from initializer list
auto b = { 1, 2.0 };
     ^   ~~~~~~~~~~~
1 error generated.
```

Another compiler gives the error below:

```
auto2.cpp:4:19: error: unable to deduce
 'std::initializer_list<_Tp>' from '{1, 2.0e+0}'
 auto b = { 1, 2.0 };
                 ^
```

Type of *a* is *std::initializer_list<int>*, i.e., *decltype(a)* is also the same.

Please note that the rules for template argument deduction is at work. For example: for determining the type of *c*

```
const auto & c = expression;
```

is the deduced type of the parameter t in the call func(expression) of the following invented function template:

```
template <class T> void func(const T& t);
```

** Question 121   scoped enumerator

Is the following program correct ?

Program 3.7: scoped enumerator

```
1 enum class Color { red, yellow, green };
2
3 int main()
4 {
5     int r = Color::red;
6
7     Color r1 = Color::red;
8
9     if (r1) { }
10 }
```

Solution of Question 121

This code doesn't get compiled. Compiler error is

```
scoped_enum1.cpp:5:9: error: cannot initialize a
variable of type 'int' with an
       rvalue of type 'Color'
    int r = Color::red;
          ^   ~~~~~~~~~~~
scoped_enum1.cpp:9:9: error: value of type
'Color' is not contextually
       convertible to 'bool'
```

```
    if (r1) { }
       ^~
2 errors generated.
```

Another compiler gives the error below:

```
scoped_enum1.cpp: In function 'int main()':
scoped_enum1.cpp:5:20: error: cannot convert
'Color' to 'int' in initialization
    int r = Color::red;
                  ^
scoped_enum1.cpp:9:11: error: could not convert
'r1' from 'Color' to 'bool'
    if (r1) { }
        ^
```

Please note that implicit enum to any other type like int or bool
conversion is not provided for a scoped enumeration.

Chapter 4

Namespaces

** Question 122   unnamed namespace

What is *unnamed namespace* ?

Solution of Question 122

An *unnamed-namespace* is a namespace without any name with potential to replace usage of static keyword.

An *unnamed-namespace-definition* behaves as if it were replaced by

```
inline namespace unique { /* empty body */ }
using namespace unique ;
namespace unique { namespace-body }
```

where inline appears if and only if it appears in the unnamed-namespace-definition, all occurrences of unique in a translation unit are replaced by the same identifier, and this identifier differs from all other identifiers in the entire program.

Although entities in an *unnamed namespace* might have external linkage, they are effectively qualified by a name unique to their translation unit and therefore can never be seen from any other translation unit.

```
namespace
{
    int a;
}

void func()
{
    ++a;
}
```

Please note that it doesn't require scope resolution operator to refer to it.

** Question 123   using unnamed namespace

What is the output of the program ?

Program 4.1: using unnamed namespace

```cpp
1 #include <iostream>
2
3 namespace A
4 {
5       namespace
6       {
7             int x;
8             int y;
9       }
10
11      void func ()
12      {
13            ++x;
14      }
15 }   // namespace A
16
17 int main ()
18 {
19      using namespace A;
20
21      A:: func () ;
22
23      ++x;
24
25      A:: x++;
26
27      ++y;
28
29      std :: cout << "x␣:␣" << x
30          << "\ny␣:␣" << y
31          << std :: endl;
```

32 }

Solution of Question 123

```
x : 3
y : 1
```

** Question 124   function defn vs unnamed namespace

Can a function declared in namespace A be defined in another namespace B ?

Program 4.2: function definition and unnamed namespace
```
1 namespace A
2 {
3     void func () ;
4 } // namespace A
5
6 namespace B
7 {
8     A:: func ()  {};
9 }
```

Solution of Question 124
No.

Compiler error is :

```
unnamed1.cpp:8:13:
error: ISO C++ forbids declaration of
'func' with no type [-fpermissive]
    A::func() {};
        ^
unnamed1.cpp:8:13:
error: declaration of 'int func()'
not in a namespace surrounding 'A'
unnamed1.cpp:8:13:
error: 'int A::func()' should have
been declared inside 'A'
unnamed1.cpp: In function 'int A::func()':
```

```
unnamed1.cpp:8:13:
error: new declaration 'int A::func()'
unnamed1.cpp:3:10:
error: ambiguates old declaration
'void A::func()'
     void func();
         ^
```

** Question 125   friend functions and namespace

Can a function declared in namespace A be defined in another namespace B ?

Program 4.3: friend functions and namespace

```
1 void func(int);
2
3 template <typename T> void g(T);
4
5 namespace A
6 {
7      struct X
8      {
9          friend void f1(X);
10
11         struct Y
12         {
13             friend void f2();
14
15             friend void func(int);
16
17             friend void g<>(int);
18         };
19     };
20
21     X x;
22
23     void f2() { f1(x); }
24
25     void f1(X) { }
26
27     void func(int) { }
28 }
29
30 int main()
31 {
32     using A::x;
33
```

```
34   A :: f1 ( x ) ;
35
36   A :: X :: f1 ( x ) ;
37
38   A :: X :: Y :: f2 ( ) ;
39 }
```

Solution of Question 125

Compiler error is :

```
namespace_friend.cpp:36:11:
error: no type named 'f1' in 'A::X'
   A::X::f1(x);
   ~~~~~~^
namespace_friend.cpp:38:14:
error: no member named 'f2' in 'A::X::Y'
   A::X::Y::f2();
   ~~~~~~~~~^
2 errors generated.
```

Another compiler gave the following error

```
namespace_friend.cpp: In function 'int main()':
namespace_friend.cpp:36:5:
error: 'f1' is not a member of 'A::X'
   A::X::f1(x);
   ^
namespace_friend.cpp:38:5:
error: 'f2' is not a member of 'A::X::Y'
   A::X::Y::f2();
   ^
```

Please note that f1 is not a member of A::X and f2 is not a member of A::X::Y.

** Question 126   namespace alias

What is namespace alias ?

Solution of Question 126

A namespace alias, say B, declares an alternate name for a given namespace, say A, like the following:

```
namespace A {}
namespace B = A;
```

Program 4.4: namespace alias

```
1 #include <cassert>
2
3 namespace long_name_123456789
4 {
5     int  i = 10;
6 } // namespace long_name_123456789
7
8 namespace short_name1 = long_name_123456789;
9
10 int  main()
11 {
12     assert(short_name1 :: i ==
13         long_name_123456789 :: i);
14 }
```

Please note that namespace alias is a synonym for the actual namespace, but when looking up a namespace-name in a namespace-alias-definition, only namespace names are considered.

Redeclaration is fine as could be seen in this program:

Program 4.5: redeclare namespace alias

```
1 #include <cassert>
2
3 namespace long_name_123456789
4 {
5     int  i = 10;
6 } // namespace long_name_123456789
7
8 namespace short_name1 = long_name_123456789;
9 namespace short_name1 = long_name_123456789;
10
11 int  main()
12 {
13     assert(short_name1 :: i ==
14         long_name_123456789 :: i);
15 }
```

Program 4.6: redeclare namespace alias

```
1 #include <cassert>
```

```
 2
 3 namespace long_name_123456789
 4 {
 5     int  i = 10;
 6 } // namespace long_name_123456789
 7
 8 namespace short_name1 = long_name_123456789;
 9 namespace short_name2 = short_name1;
10 namespace short_name2 = short_name2;
11
12 int  main()
13 {
14     assert(short_name1::i ==
15         long_name_123456789::i);
16 }
```

But redefinition is not allowed:

Program 4.7: redefinition namespace alias

```
 1 #include <cassert>
 2
 3 namespace long_name_1 {};
 4 namespace long_name_2 {};
 5
 6 namespace A = long_name_1;
 7 namespace A = long_name_2;
```

This program doesn't get compiled, the error is:

```
namespace_alias3.cpp:7:11:
error: redefinition of 'A' as different kind of
    symbol
namespace A = long_name_2;
          ^
namespace_alias3.cpp:6:11:
note: previous definition is here
namespace A = long_name_1;
          ^

1 error generated
```

** Question 127   using declaration

In this program, which functions will be called by the member functions of the class Derived ?

Program 4.8: using declaration

```
1 struct Base
2 {
3      void f1 (char) ;
4
5      void f2 (char) ;
6 };
7
8 struct Derived : Base
9 {
10     using Base :: f1 ;
11
12     void f1 (int)
13     {
14          f1 ( 'a' ) ;
15     }
16
17     void f2 (int)
18     {
19          f2 ( 'a' ) ;
20     }
21 };
```

Solution of Question 127

- Line 14 calls Base::f1(char)

- Line 19 recursively calls Derived::f2(int);

*** Question 128   using declaration and base class

Can using declaration be used to refer to a non-base class member function as seen the program ?

Program 4.9: using declaration and base class

```
1 struct Base
2 {
3      void f1 () ;
4 };
5
6 struct Test
7 {
8      void f2 () ;
9 };
10
11 struct Derived : Base
12 {
```

```
13    using Base :: f1 ;
14    using Test :: f2 ;
15 } ;
```

Solution of Question 128

No. This program results into a compiler error :

```
using2.cpp:14:11:
error: using declaration refers into
'Test::', which is not a
      base class of 'Derived'
    using Test::f2;
          ^~~~~~
1 error generated.
```

*** **Question 129**   using declaration and template-id

What is problem with this code ?

Program 4.10: using declaration and template-id

```
1 struct A
2 {
3     template <typename T> void func(T);
4
5     template <typename T> struct B { };
6 };
7
8 struct B : A
9 {
10    using A::func<double>;
11
12    using A::B<int >;
13 };
```

Solution of Question 129

This program results into a compiler error :

```
using3.cpp:10:14:
error: using declaration can not refer
to a template
        specialization
```

```
        using A::func<double>;
            ^       ~~~~~~~~
using3.cpp:12:14:
error: using declaration can not refer
to a template
        specialization
        using A::B<int>;
              ^~~~~
2 errors generated.
```

The reason is simple : a using-declaration cannot be used to name a template-id.

*** Question 130   using declaration and member decl

What is problem with this code ?

Program 4.11: using declaration and member declaration
```
1 struct A
2 {
3     int i;
4     static int si;
5 };
6
7 void f()
8 {
9     using A::i;
10    using A::si;
11 }
```

Solution of Question 130

This program results into a compiler error :

```
using4.cpp:9:14:
error: using declaration can not refer to
class member
    using A::i;
          ~~~^
using4.cpp:10:14:
error: using declaration can not refer to
class member
    using A::si;
```

```
      ~~~^
2 errors generated.
```

With another compiler, the error is:

```
using4.cpp: In function 'void f()':
using4.cpp:9:14: error: 'A' is not a namespace
    using A::i;
             ^
using4.cpp:10:14: error: 'A' is not a namespace
    using A::si;
              ^
```

A using-declaration for a class member should be a member-declaration.

A::i is a class member and this is not a member declaration.
A::si is a class member and this is not a member declaration.
Hence the error.

** Question 131   using declaration and refer members

Review the code below.

Program 4.12: using declaration and referring members

```
 1 void  f ( ) ;
 2
 3 namespace  A
 4 {
 5      void  g ( ) ;
 6 }
 7
 8 namespace  B
 9 {
10      using  :: f ;
11      using  A:: g ;
12 }
13
14 void  h ( )
15 {
16      B:: f ( ) ;
17      B:: g ( ) ;
18 }
```

Solution of Question 131

In namespace B, *using ::f* calls the global f. *using A::g calls A'g.*

In the function h(), *B::f()* calls the global f. *B::g()* calls A::g.

In short, members declared by a using-declaration can be referred to by explicit qualification just like other member names and in a using-declaration, a prefix *::* refers to the global namespace.

*** Question 132   multiple using declaration

Review the code below.

Program 4.13: multiple using declaration

```
1 namespace A
2 {
3     int i;
4 }
5
6 namespace A1
7 {
8     using A::i;
9     using A::i;
10 }
11
12 void f()
13 {
14     using A::i;
15     using A::i;
16 }
17
18 struct B
19 {
20     int i;
21 };
22
23 struct X : B
24 {
25     using B::i;
26     using B::i;
27 };
```

Solution of Question 132

Compiler error is:

```
using6.cpp: In function 'void f()':
using6.cpp:15:14:
error: 'i' is already declared in this
scope
     using A::i;
              ^
using6.cpp: At global scope:
using6.cpp:26:14:
error: redeclaration of 'using B::i'
     using B::i;
              ^
using6.cpp:25:14:
note: previous declaration 'using B::i'
     using B::i;
              ^
```

A using-declaration is a declaration and can therefore be used repeatedly where (and only where) multiple declarations are allowed.

In this code, in namespace *A1*, second occurrence of *using A::i* is a valid double declaration, whereas the in void f, *using A::i* and in struct X, *using B::i* : is invalid case of double member declaration.

*** **Question 133   availability of using declaration**

Review the code below.

Program 4.14: availability of using declaration

```
1 namespace A
2 {
3      void  f(int);
4 }
5
6 using A::f;
7
8 namespace A
9 {
10      void  f(char);
11 }
12
13 void  foo()
14 {
15      f('a');
```

```
16 }
17
18 void  bar ()
19 {
20       using  A:: f ;
21       f ( 'a' ) ;
22 }
```

Solution of Question 133

First occurrence of *using A::f;* in global namespace marks *f* as a synonym for *A::f*, that is, for *A::f(int)*.

f('a') in *void foo()* calls *f(int)*, even though *f(char)* exists.

in the function *void bar()*, *using A::f* marks *f* as a synonym for *A::f*, that is, for *A::f(int)* and *A::f(char)* and *f('a')* calls *f(char)*.

The entity declared by a using-declaration should be known in the context using it according to its definition at the point of the using-declaration. Definitions added to the namespace after the using-declaration are not considered when a use of the name is made.

*** Question 134   using declaration and same functions

Review the code below.

Program 4.15: using declaration and same functions

```
 1 namespace  B
 2 {
 3       void  f ( int ) ;
 4       void  f ( double ) ;
 5 }
 6
 7 namespace  C
 8 {
 9       void  f ( int ) ;
10       void  f ( double ) ;
11       void  f ( char ) ;
12 }
13
14 void  h ()
15 {
16       using  B:: f ;
17       using  C:: f ;
18       f ( 'h' ) ;
19       f ( 1 ) ;
```

20   **void** f (**int**) ;
21 }

Solution of Question 134

Compiler error is:

```
using8.cpp:19:5: error: call to 'f' is ambiguous
    f(1);
    ^

using8.cpp:3:10: note: candidate function
    void f(int);
         ^

using8.cpp:9:10: note: candidate function
    void f(int);
         ^

using8.cpp:4:10: note: candidate function
    void f(double);
         ^

using8.cpp:10:10: note: candidate function
    void f(double);
         ^

using8.cpp:11:10: note: candidate function
    void f(char);
         ^

using8.cpp:20:10:
error: declaration conflicts with target
of using declaration
      already in scope
    void f(int);
         ^

using8.cpp:9:10: note: target of using declaration
    void f(int);
         ^

using8.cpp:17:14: note: using declaration
    using C::f;
           ^

2 errors generated.
```

- If a function declaration in namespace scope or block scope has the same name and the same parameter-type-list as a function introduced by a using-declaration, and the declarations do not declare the same function, the program is ill-formed.

- If a function template declaration in namespace scope has the same name, parameter-type-list, return type, and template parameter list as a function template introduced by a using-declaration, the program is ill-formed.

- Two using-declarations may introduce functions with the same name and the same parameter-type-list. If, for a call to an unqualified function name, function overload resolution selects the functions introduced by such using-declarations, the function call is ill-formed.

So, in the function *void h()*

- *using B::f;* denotes both *B::f(int)* and *B::f(double)*

- *using C::f;* denotes *C::f(int)*, *C::f(double)*, and *C::f(char)*

- *f('h')* calls *C::f(char)*

- *f(1)* is a ambiguous call : *B::f(int)* or *C::f(int)* ?

- *void f(int)* conflixt with *C::f(int)* and *B::f(int)*.

*** **Question 135**   **hide/override and using declaration**

Review the code below.

Program 4.16: hide/override and using declaration

```
1 struct B
2 {
3      virtual void f(int);
4      virtual void f(char);
5      void g(int);
6      void h(int);
7 };
8
9 struct D : B
10 {
11     using B::f;
12     void f(int);
13     using B::g;
14     void g(char);
15     using B::h;
```

```
16        void  h ( int ) ;
17 } ;
18
19 void  k ( D*  p )
20 {
21        p->f ( 1 ) ;
22        p->f ( ' a ' ) ;
23        p->g ( 1 ) ;
24        p->g ( ' a ' ) ;
25 }
```

Solution of Question 135

When a using-declaration brings names from a base class into a derived class scope, member functions and member function templates in the derived class override and/or hide member functions and member function templates with the same name, parameter-type-list, cv-qualification, and ref-qualifier (if any) in a base class (rather than conflicting).

In the code, in struct D:

- *void f(int) is ok because D::f(int) overrides B::f(int).*

- *void g(char) is ok, it is just another overloaded function.*

- *void h(int) is also ok because D::h(int) hides B::h(int).*

In the function *void k(D* p)*:

- *p->f(1) calls D::f(int)*

- *p->f('a') calls B::f(char)*

- *p->g(1) calls B::g(int)*

- *p->g('a') calls D::g(char)*

*** **Question 136**   **using declaration and ambiguous base**

In this program, which function will be called by *d->x()*?

Program 4.17: using declaration and ambiguous base

```
1 struct  A
2 {
3        int  x ( ) ;
4 } ;
5
```

```
 6 struct B : A { };
 7
 8 struct C : A
 9 {
10     using A::x;
11     int x(int);
12 };
13
14 struct D : B, C
15 {
16     using C::x;
17     int x(double);
18 };
19
20 int f(D* d)
21 {
22     return d->x();
23 }
```

Solution of Question 136

This program doesn't get compiled. The compiler error is:

```
using10.cpp:22:12: error: ambiguous conversion from
derived class 'D' to base class 'A':
    struct D -> struct B -> struct A
    struct D -> struct C -> struct A
    return d->x();
           ^

1 error generated.
```

Another compiler gave the following error:

```
using10.cpp: In function 'int f(D*)':
using10.cpp:22:17:
error: 'A' is an ambiguous base of 'D'
     return d->x();
            ^
```

If a derived class uses a using-declaration to access a member of a base class, the member name is accessible. If the name is that of an overloaded member function, then all functions named are accessible. The base class members mentioned by a

using-declaration is visible in the scope of at least one of the
direct base classes of the class where the using-declaration is
specified. Because a using-declaration designates a base class
member (and not a member subobject or a member function of
a base class subobject), a using-declaration cannot be used to
resolve inherited member ambiguities.

That's why $d->x()$ is an ambiguous call : $B::x$ or $C::x$?

*** Question 137   using declaration and access

Review the program.

Program 4.18: using declaration and accessibility rules

```
1  class A
2  {
3  private:
4      void  f(char);
5
6  public:
7      void  f(int);
8
9  protected:
10     void  g();
11 };
12
13 class B : public A
14 {
15     using A::f;
16
17 public:
18     using A::g;
19 };
```

Solution of Question 137

This program doesn't get compiled. The compiler error is:

```
using11.cpp:15:14:
error: 'f' is a private member of 'A'
    using A::f;
             ^

using11.cpp:4:10: note: declared private here
    void f(char);
         ^
```

The alias created by the using-declaration has the usual accessibility for a member declaration.

** Question 138   using directive

Review the program.

Program 4.19: using directive

```
 1 namespace A
 2 {
 3     int i;
 4
 5     namespace B
 6     {
 7         namespace C
 8         {
 9             int i;
10         } // namespace C
11
12         using namespace A::B::C;
13
14         void f1()
15         {
16             i = 5;
17         }
18     } // namespace B
19
20     namespace D
21     {
22         using namespace B;
23         using namespace C;
24
25         void f2()
26         {
27             i = 5;
28         }
29     } // namespace D
30
31     void f3()
32     {
33         i = 5;
34     }
35 } // namespace A
36
37 void f4()
38 {
39     i = 5;
40 }
```

Solution of Question 138

This program doesn't get compiled. The compiler error is:

```
using12.cpp:27:13:
error: reference to 'i' is ambiguous
            i = 5;
            ^
using12.cpp:3:9:
note: candidate found by name lookup is
'A::i'
      int i;
          ^
using12.cpp:9:17:
note: candidate found by name lookup is
'A::B::C::i'
                int i;
                    ^
using12.cpp:39:5:
error: use of undeclared identifier 'i';
did you mean 'A::i'?
      i = 5;
      ^
      A::i
using12.cpp:3:9: note: 'A::i' declared here
      int i;
          ^
2 errors generated.
```

A using-directive does not add any members to the declarative region in which it appears. Hence,

- in f1, $i = 5$ is ok, $C::i$ is visible in B and hides $A::i$

- in f2, $i = 5$ is ambiguous, $B::C::i$ or $A::i$?

- in f3, $i = 5$ uses $A::i$

- in f4, $i = 5$ is ill-formed; neither i is visible

Chapter 5

Misc

** Question 139   nested linkage specifications

Review the program.

Program 5.1: nested linkage specifications
```
1 extern "C" void f1 ( void ( * pf ) ( int ) ) ;
2
3 extern "C" typedef void FUNC( ) ;
4 FUNC f2 ;
5
6 extern "C" FUNC f3 ;
7
8 void ( * pf2 ) ( FUNC* ) ;
9
10 extern "C"
11 {
12     static void f4 ( ) ;
13 }
14
15 extern "C" void f5 ( )
16 {
17     extern void f4 ( ) ;
18 }
19
20 extern void f4 ( ) ;
21
22 void f6 ( )
23 {
24     extern void f4 ( ) ;
25 }
```

Solution of Question 139

- *f1*: The name f1 and its function type have C language linkage; pf is a pointer to a C function

- *f2*: The name f2 has C++ language linkage and the function's type has C language linkage.

- *f3*: The name of function f3 and the function's type have C language linkage. The name of the variable pf2 has C++ linkage and the type of pf2 is pointer to C++ function that takes one parameter of type pointer to C function.

- *f4*: The name of the function f4 has internal linkage (not C language linkage) and the function's type has C language linkage.

- *f5*: Name linkage (internal) and function type linkage (C language linkage) gotten from previous declaration.

Linkage specifications nest. When linkage specifications nest, the innermost one determines the language linkage.

A linkage specification does not establish a scope. A linkage-specification occurs only in namespace scope.

In a linkage-specification, the specified language linkage applies to the function types of all function declarators, function names with external linkage, and variable names with external linkage declared within the linkage-specification.

*** Question 140   alignment specifier

What is alignment specifier(s)?

Solution of Question 140

An alignment-specifier may be applied to a variable or to a class data member, but it can not be applied to a bit-field, a function parameter, the formal parameter of a catch clause, or a variable declared with the register storage class specifier. An alignment-specifier may also be applied to the declaration of a class or enumeration type. An alignment-specifier with an ellipsis is a pack expansion.

When the alignment-specifier is of the form **alignas**(*assignment-expression*):

- the assignment-expression should be an integral constant expression

- if the constant expression evaluates to a fundamental alignment, the alignment requirement of the declared entity is the specified fundamental alignment

- if the constant expression evaluates to an extended alignment and the implementation supports that alignment in the context of the declaration, the alignment of the declared entity should be that alignment

- if the constant expression evaluates to an extended alignment and the implementation does not support that alignment in the context of the declaration, the program is ill-formed

- if the constant expression evaluates to zero, the alignment specifier has no effect

- otherwise, the program is ill-formed.

When the alignment-specifier is of the form **alignas**(*type-id*), it has the same effect as **alignas**(**alignof**(*type-id*)).

When multiple alignment-specifiers are specified for an entity, the alignment requirement should be set to the strictest specified alignment.

The combined effect of all alignment-specifiers in a declaration should not specify an alignment that is less strict than the alignment that would be required for the entity being declared if all alignment-specifiers were omitted (including those in other declarations). If the defining declaration of an entity has an alignment-specifier, any non-defining declaration of that entity shall either specify equivalent alignment or have no alignment-specifier. Conversely, if any declaration of an entity has an alignment-specifier, every defining declaration of that entity shall specify an equivalent alignment. No diagnostic is required if declarations of an entity have different alignment-specifiers in different translation units.

If the defining declaration of an entity has an alignment-specifier, any non-defining declaration of that entity should either specify equivalent alignment or have no alignment-specifier. Conversely, if any declaration of an entity has an alignment-specifier, every defining declaration of that entity should specify an equivalent alignment. No diagnostic is required if declarations of an entity have different alignment-specifiers in different translation units.

For example:

```
1 // Translation unit #1:
2 struct S { int x; } s, p = &s;
3
4
5 // Translation unit #2:
6 // error: definition of S lacks alignment;
7 // no diagnostic required
8 struct alignas(16) S;
9 extern S* p;
```

An aligned buffer with an alignment requirement of A and holding N elements of type T other than char, signed char, or unsigned char can be declared as:

$$alignas(T)\ alignas(A)\ T\ buffer[N];$$

Specifying *alignas*(T) ensures that the final requested alignment will not be weaker than *alignof*(T), and therefore the program will not be ill-formed.

```
1 // error: alignment applied to function
2 alignas(double) void f();
3
4 // array of characters, suitably aligned for
      a double
5 alignas(double) unsigned char c[sizeof(double
      )];
6
7 // no alignas necessary
8 extern unsigned char c[sizeof(double)];
9
10 // error: different alignment in declaration
11 alignas(float) extern unsigned char c[sizeof(
      double)];
```

*** Question 141   noreturn attribute

Review the program below.

Program 5.2: noreturn attribute
```
1 [[ noreturn ]] void f()
2 {
3     throw "error";
4 }
5
```

```
 6 [[ noreturn ]] void q(int i)
 7 {
 8     if (i > 0)
 9     throw "positive";
10 }
```

Solution of Question 141

The compiler issues a warning:

```
noreturn.cpp:10:1:
warning: function declared 'noreturn'
should not return
        [-Winvalid-noreturn]

1 warning generated.
```

The attribute-token *noreturn* specifies that a function does not return. It appears at most once in each attribute-list and no attribute-argument-clause is present. The attribute may be applied to the declarator-id in a function declaration. The first declaration of a function specifies the *noreturn* attribute if any declaration of that function specifies the *noreturn* attribute.

If a function is declared with the *noreturn* attribute in one translation unit and the same function is declared without the *noreturn* attribute in another translation unit, the program is ill-formed.

If a function f is called where f was previously declared with the *noreturn* attribute and f eventually returns, the behavior is undefined. The function may terminate by throwing an exception.

*** Question 142   carriage_dependency attribute

What is *carriage_dependency* attribute ?

Solution of Question 142

The attribute-token *carries_dependency* specifies dependency propagation into and out of functions. It appears at most once in each attribute-list and no attribute-argument-clause is present. The attribute may be applied to the declarator-id of a parameter-declaration in a function declaration or lambda, in which case it specifies that the initialization of the parameter carries a dependency to each lvalue-to-rvalue conversion of that object. The attribute may also be applied to the declarator-id of a function declaration, in which case it specifies that the return value, if any, carries a dependency to the evaluation of the function call expression.

The first declaration of a function will specify the *carries_dependency* attribute for its declarator-id if any declaration of the function specifies the *carries_dependency* attribute. Furthermore, the first declaration of a function shall specify the *carries_dependency* attribute for a parameter if any declaration of that function specifies the *carries_dependency* attribute for that parameter. If a function or one of its parameters is declared with the *carries_dependency* attribute in its first declaration in one translation unit and the same function or one of its parameters is declared without the *carries_dependency* attribute in its first declaration in another translation unit, the program is ill-formed.

The *carries_dependency* attribute does not change the meaning of the program, but may result in generation of more efficient code.

For example:

```cpp
1 // Translation unit A.
2
3 struct foo { int* a; int* b; };
4
5 std::atomic<struct foo *> foo_head[10];
6
7 int foo_array[10][10];
8
9 [[carries_dependency]] struct foo* f(int i)
10 {
11     return foo_head[i].load(
            memory_order_consume);
12 }
13
14 [[carries_dependency]] int g(int* x, int* y)
15 {
16     return kill_dependency(foo_array[*x][*y])
            ;
17 }
18
19
20 // Translation unit B.
21 [[carries_dependency]] struct foo* f(int i);
22
```

```
23 [[carries_dependency]] int* g(int* x, int* y)
       ;
24
25 int c = 3;
26
27 void h(int i)
28 {
29     struct foo* p;
30     p = f(i);
31     do_something_with(g(&c, p->a));
32     do_something_with(g(p->a, &c));
33 }
```

The *carries_dependency* attribute on function f means that the return value carries a dependency out of f, so that the implementation need not constrain ordering upon return from f. Implementations of f and its caller may choose to preserve dependencies instead of emitting hardware memory ordering instructions(a.k.a. fences).

Function g's second argument has a *carries_dependency* attribute, but its first argument does not. Therefore, function h's first call to g carries a dependency into g, but its second call does not. The implementation might need to insert a fence prior to the second call to g.

*** Question 143   auto as trailing return type

What is the meaning of the code fragment given below?

```
1 auto f()->int(*)[4];
```

Solution of Question 143

It is a function returning a pointer to array[4] of int, not a function returning array[4] of pointer to int.

** Question 144   parameter type of function

What is the type of the parameter to the function f below?

```
1 class A { };
2 void f(int(A)) { }
```

Solution of Question 144

It is equivalent to

```
1 void f(int(*fp)(A a)) { }
```

not

```
1 void f(int A) { }
```

** Question 145   parameter type of function

What is the type of the parameter to the function f below?

```
1 class A { };
2 void f(int *(A[10]));
```

Solution of Question 145

It is equivalent to

```
1 void f(int *(*fp)(A a[10]));
```

not

```
1 void f(int *A[10]);
```

** Question 146   pointers

Review the program.

Program 5.3: pointers

```
 1 int main()
 2 {
 3     const int ci = 10, *pc = &ci, *const cpc
           = pc, **ppc;
 4
 5     int i, *p, *const cp = &i;
 6
 7     i = ci;
 8     *cp = ci;
 9     pc++;
10     pc = cpc;
11     pc = p;
12     ppc = &pc;
13
14     ci = 1;
15     ci++;
16     *pc = 2;
17     cp = &ci;
18     cpc++;
19     p = pc;
20     ppc = &p;
21 }
```

Solution of Question 146

It declares

- ci, a constant integer;

- pc, a pointer to a constant integer;

- cpc, a constant pointer to a constant integer;

- ppc, a pointer to a pointer to a constant integer;

- i, an integer;

- p, a pointer to integer; and

- cp, a constant pointer to integer.

The value of ci, cpc, and cp cannot be changed after initialization. The value of pc can be changed, and so can the object pointed to by cp.

Each of the first six are examples of correct operations, whereas the rest are illegal operations resulting into the following compiler error

```
pointers.cpp:14:8:
error: read-only variable is not assignable
    ci = 1;
    ~~ ^
pointers.cpp:15:7:
error: read-only variable is not assignable
    ci++;
    ~~^
pointers.cpp:16:9:
error: read-only variable is not assignable
    *pc = 2;
    ~~~ ^
pointers.cpp:17:8:
error: read-only variable is not assignable
    cp = &ci;
    ~~ ^
pointers.cpp:18:8:
error: read-only variable is not assignable
    cpc++;
    ~~~^
pointers.cpp:19:7:
error: assigning to 'int *' from incompatible type
        'const int *'
```

```
    p = pc;
    ^  ~~
pointers.cpp:20:9:
error: assigning to 'const int **' from
incompatible type
        'int **'
    ppc = &p;
          ^ ~~
7 errors generated.
```

Each is unacceptable because it would either change the value
of an object declared const or allow it to be changed through a
cv-unqualified pointer later, for example:

1 *ppc = &ci ;

is OK, but would make p point to ci because of previous error

1 *p = 5;

clobbers ci.

** Question 147   lvalue reference

Review the program.

1 typedef int& A;
2 const A aref = 3;

Solution of Question 147

The program is ill-formed because lvalue reference to non-
const is initialized with rvalue. The type of aref is *lvalue reference to int*, not *lvalue reference to const int*.

Please note that a reference can be thought of as a name of an
object and a declarator that specifies the type *reference to cv
void* is ill-formed too.

** Question 148   types

What are the types of the variables r1, r2, r3, r4, r5, r6 and
r7 in the following program ?

Program 5.4: types

1 int i;
2 typedef int& LRI;
3 typedef int&& RRI;
4

```
5 LRI& r1 = i;
6 const LRI& r2 = i;
7 const LRI&& r3 = i;
8
9 RRI& r4 = i;
10 RRI&& r5 = 5;
11
12 decltype(r2)& r6 = i;
13 decltype(r2)&& r7 = i;
```

Solution of Question 148

All have the type *int&* because if a typedef, a type template-parameter, or a decltype-specifier denotes a type *TR*, that is a reference to a type T, an attempt to create the type *lvalue reference to cv TR* creates the type *lvalue reference to T*, while an attempt to create the type *rvalue reference to cv TR* creates the type *TR*.

** Question 149   pointers to members

Review the program below.

Program 5.5: pointers to members
```
1 struct X
2 {
3     void f(int);
4     int a;
5 };
6
7 struct Y;
8
9 int X::* pmi = &X::a;
10 void (X::* pmf)(int) = &X::f;
11 double X::* pmd;
12 char Y::* pmc;
13
14 int main()
15 {
16     X obj;
17
18     obj.*pmi = 7;
19     (obj.*pmf)(7);
20 }
```

Solution of Question 149

It declares *pmi, pmf, pmd* and *pmc* to be a pointer to a member of X of type *int*, a pointer to a member of X of type *void(int)*, a pointer to a member of X of type *double* and a pointer to a member of *Y* of type *char* respectively.

The declaration of *pmd* is well-formed even though *X* has no members of type *double*.

Similarly, the declaration of *pmc* is well-formed even though *Y* is an incomplete type. *pmi* and *pmf* can be used like shown in the program.

** Question 150   arrays and typedef

What are the types of *CA* and *CAA*?

```
1 typedef int A[5] , AA[2][3];
2 typedef const A CA;
3 typedef const AA CAA;
```

Solution of Question 150

- *CA* denotes a type of *array of 5 const int.*

- *CAA* denotes a type of *array of 2 array of 3 const int.*

** Question 151   arrays and sizeof

What is the output of the program?

Program 5.6: arrays and sizeof

```
1 #include <iostream>
2
3 extern int x[10];
4
5 struct S
6 {
7     static int y[20];
8 };
9
10 int x[];
11 int S::y[];
12
13 void f()
14 {
15     std::cout << sizeof(x)/sizeof(int) << std
           ::endl;
16 }
17
18 void g()
19 {
```

```
20      std :: cout  <<  sizeof(S :: y)/sizeof(int)  <<
           std :: endl;
21 }
22
23 void  h()
24 {
25      extern  int  x[];
26      std :: cout  <<  sizeof(x)/sizeof(int)  <<  std
              :: endl;
27 }
28
29 int  main()
30 {
31      f();
32      g();
33      h();
34 }
```

Solution of Question 151

The program doesn't compile because the function h calls *sizeof* on the incomplete object type x.

If the function h is omitted the the rest of the program prints *10* and *20* respectively.

** Question 152   type of function

Is the following statement true?

The type of the functions denoted by

```
1 int (*)(const  int  p,  decltype(p)*)
```

is same as that by

```
1 int (*)(int ,  const  int *)
```

Solution of Question 152

Yes. Because the type of a function is determined using the following rules:

- The type of each parameter (including function parameter packs) is determined from its own *decl-specifier-seq* and *declarator*.

- After determining the type of each parameter, any parameter of type *array of T* or *function returning T* is adjusted to be *pointer to T* or *pointer to function returning T*, respectively.

- After producing the list of parameter types, any top-level *cv-qualifiers* modifying a parameter type are deleted when forming the function type.

- The resulting list of transformed parameter types and the presence or absence of the ellipsis or a function parameter pack is the function's *parameter-type-list*.

Please note that this transformation does not affect the types of the parameters.

** Question 153   type of member function

What is the type of the member function *f* ?

```
1 typedef void F();
2
3 struct A
4 {
5     const F f;
6 };
```

Solution of Question 153

It is equivalent to *void f();*

** Question 154   typedef and function definition

What is problem with this code snippet ?

Program 5.7: typedef and function definition
```
1 typedef void F();
2 F fv;
3 F fv { }
4 void fv() { }
```

Solution of Question 154

Compiler error is:

```
typedef.cpp:3:3: error: illegal initializer
(only variables can be initialized)
F fv { }
  ^
typedef.cpp:3:9:
error: expected ';' after top level declarator
```

```
F fv { }
       ^

       ;
2 errors generated.
```

The reason is simple : A typedef of function type may be used
to declare a function but can not be used to define a function.

- F fv: is ok, it is equivalent to *void fv();*

- F fv{ }: is ill-formed

- void fv() { }: is also ok because it is definition of *fv*

*** Question 155   typedef and const volatile function

What is problem with this code snippet ?

Program 5.8: typedef and const volatile function
```
1 typedef int FIC(int) const;
2
3 FIC f;
4
5 struct A
6 {
7     FIC f;
8 };
9
10 FIC A::*pm = &A::f;
```

Solution of Question 155

Compiler error is:

```
typedef1.cpp:3:1:
error: non-member function of type 'FIC'
      (aka 'int (int) const') cannot have 'const'
      qualifier
FIC f;
^

1 error generated.
```

The reason is : A typedef of a function type whose declarator
includes a cv-qualifier-seq can be used only

- to declare the function type for a non-static member function,

- to declare the function type to which a pointer to member refers, or

- to declare the top-level function type of another function typedef declaration.

So *FC f* is ille-formed because it does not declare a member function.

****** Question 156**   **trailing return types**

Declare a function template *add* which takes two parameters of different types and returns the sum of the arguments passed.

Solution of Question 156

```
1 template <typename T, typename U>
2 auto add(T t, U u) -> decltype(t + u);
```

Alternative is:

```
1 template <typename T, typename U>
2 decltype((*(T*)0) + (*(U*)0)) add(T t, U u);
```

****** Question 157**   **trailing return types**

Declare a function *f* so that we can write the following code:

```
1 int add(int, int);
2
3 float subtract(int, int);
4
5 void g()
6 {
7     f(add, subtract);
8 }
```

Solution of Question 157

```
1 template<typename... T>
2 void f(T (* ...t)(int, int));
```

***** Question 158**   **default argument**

What is the output of this program?

Program 5.9: default argument

```
1 #include <iostream>
2
3 int  a = 1;
4
5 int  f(int  i)
6 {
7      return i;
8 }
9
10 int  g(int  x = f(a))
11 {
12      return x;
13 }
14
15 void  h()
16 {
17      a = 2;
18      {
19          int  a = 3;
20          std::cout << g() << std::endl;
21      }
22 }
23
24 int  main()
25 {
26      h();
27 }
```

Solution of Question 158

It prints *2*.

Because the default argument of the function g is *f(::a)* and *::a*
becomes 2 here.

*** Question 159   **default argument and member function**

Review the program.

```
1 class A
2 {
3      void  f(int  i = 3);
4      void  g(int  i, int  j = 99);
5 };
6
7 void A::f(int  i = 3)
8 {
9 }
10
11 void A::g(int  i = 88, int  j)
```

```
12 {
13 }
```

Solution of Question 159

void A::f(int i = 3) is ill-formed because default argument is already specified in class cope.

void A::g(int i = 88, int j) is ok, in this translation unit, A::g can be called with no argument.

Except for member functions of class templates, the default arguments in a member function definition that appears outside of the class definition are added to the set of default arguments provided by the member function declaration in the class definition.

Default arguments for a member function of a class template will be specified on the initial declaration of the member function within the class template.

*** Question 160   default argument and local variables

Is this program valid?

Program 5.10: default argument and local variables
```
1 void f ()
2 {
3     int i;
4     extern void g(int x = i);
5 }
```

Solution of Question 160

No because local variables can not be used in a default argument.

Compiler error is:

```
default1.cpp:4:27:
error: default argument references local variable
'i' of
      enclosing function
    extern void g(int x = i);
                          ^
1 error generated.
```

*** Question 161   default argument and this

Is this program valid?

```
1 class A
2 {
3     void f(A* p = this) { }
4 };
```

Solution of Question 161

No because the keyword *this* can not be used in a default argument of a member function.

*** Question 162   explicitly defaulted functions

Is this program valid?

Program 5.11: explicitly defaulted functions

```
1 struct A
2 {
3     constexpr A() = default;
4
5     A(int a = 0) = default;
6
7     void operator=(const A&) = default;
8
9     ~A() throw(int) = default;
10
11 private:
12     int i;
13     A(A&);
14 };
15
16 A::A(A&) = default;
```

Solution of Question 162

? *No.* The compiler error is

```
explicit_default.cpp:3:5:
error: defaulted definition of default constructor
  is not constexpr
    constexpr A() = default;
    ^

explicit_default.cpp:5:5:
error: an explicitly-defaulted constructor cannot
```

```
have default arguments
    A(int a = 0) = default;
    ^~~~~~~~~~~~~
explicit_default.cpp:7:10:
error: explicitly-defaulted
copy assignment operator
      must return 'A &'
    void operator=(const A&) = default;
         ^
explicit_default.cpp:9:5:
error: exception specification of
explicitly defaulted
      destructor does not match the calculated one
    ~A() throw(int) = default;
    ^
4 errors generated.
```

- *constexpr A() = default;* is ill-formed because implicit A() is not constexpr

- *A (int a = 0) = default;* is ill-formed because of the present of default argument

- *void operator=(const A&) = default;* is ill-formed because of non-matching return type

- *A() throw(int) = default;* is ill-formed because exception specification does not match.

*** Question 163   prevent new instance of class

How to design a class such that its instance cannot be dynamically allocated with *new* ?

Solution of Question 163

One can prevent use of a class in certain new expressions by using deleted definitions of a user-declared operator new for that class as shown below.

Program 5.12: prevent new instance of class

```
1 #include <cstddef>
2
3 struct A
4 {
```

```
5    void *operator new(std::size_t) = delete;
6    void *operator new[](std::size_t) =
         delete;
7  };
8
9  int main()
10 {
11     A *p = new A;
12     A *q = new A[3];
13 }
```

Compiler error is

```
new_deleted.cpp:11:12:
error: call to deleted function 'operator new'
    A *p = new A;
           ^
new_deleted.cpp:5:11:
note: candidate function has been
explicitly deleted
    void *operator new(std::size_t) = delete;
          ^
new_deleted.cpp:12:12:
error: call to deleted function 'operator new[]'
    A *q = new A[3];
           ^
new_deleted.cpp:6:11:
note: candidate function has been
explicitly deleted
    void *operator new[](std::size_t) = delete;
          ^
2 errors generated.
```

*** Question 164   noncopyable (aka moveonly) class

How to design a noncopyable, i.e., moveonly class?

Solution of Question 164

Program 5.13: noncopyable (aka moveonly) class

```
1  struct moveonly
2  {
3      moveonly() = default;
```

```
4      moveonly(const moveonly&) = delete;
5      moveonly(moveonly&&) = default;
6
7      moveonly& operator=(const moveonly&) =
           delete;
8      moveonly& operator=(moveonly&&) = default
           ;
9
10     ~moveonly() = default;
11 };
12
13 int main()
14 {
15     moveonly *p;
16     moveonly q(*p);
17 }
```

Compiler error is

```
moveonly.cpp:16:14:
error: call to deleted constructor of 'moveonly'
    moveonly q(*p);
              ^ ~~
moveonly.cpp:4:5:
note: function has been explicitly marked
deleted here
    moveonly(const moveonly&) = delete;
    ^

1 error generated.
```

** Question 165   deleted function and inline

What is the problem with this code?

Program 5.14: deleted function and inline

```
1 struct A
2 {
3     A();
4 };
5
6 A::A() = delete;
```

Solution of Question 165

Compiler error is

```
deleted.cpp:6:10:
error: deleted definition must be first declaration
A::A() = delete;
       ^

deleted.cpp:3:5: note: previous declaration is here
   A();
   ^

1 error generated.
```

A deleted function is implicitly *inline*. Please note that the one-definition rule applies to deleted definitions as well. A deleted definition of a function is the first declaration of the function or, for an explicit specialization of a function template, the first declaration of that specialization.

**** Question 166   static member initialization scope

What is the output of this program?

Program 5.15: static member initialization scope
```cpp
#include <iostream>

int a = 10;

struct X
{
    static int a;
    static int b;
};

int X::a = 20;
int X::b = a;

int main()
{
    std::cout << X::b << std::endl;
}
```

Solution of Question 166

It prints *20*.

Because an initializer for a static member is in the scope of the member's class.

Hence the following two are equivalent:

```
1 int  X::b = a;
```

```
1 int  X::b = X::a;
```

** Question 167   initializer list

How to initialize the variables a.x, a.b.i and a.b.j with the values 1, 2 and 3 respectively, using an initializer list?

```
1 struct  A
2 {
3     int  x;
4
5     struct  B
6     {
7         int  i;
8         int  j;
9     } b;
10 } a;
```

Solution of Question 167

```
1 struct  A
2 {
3     int  x;
4
5     struct  B
6     {
7         int  i;
8         int  j;
9     } b;
10 } a = { 1, { 2, 3 } };
```

** Question 168   initializer list and map

Initialize *std::map<std::string, int>* with 3 pairs as ("One", 1), ("Two", 2) and ("Three", 3) respectively.

Solution of Question 168

Program 5.16: initializer list and map
```
1 std::map<std::string, int> m =
2     { {"One", 1}, {"Two", 2}, {"Three", 3} };
```

* Question 169   initializer list and constructor

What is the output of the program?

Program 5.17: initializer list and constructor

```cpp
#include <initializer_list>
#include <iostream>

struct A
{
    A(std::initializer_list <double>)
    {
        std::cout << "Inside A(std::
            initializer_list <double>)" << std
            ::endl;
    }

    A(std::initializer_list <int>)
    {
        std::cout << "Inside A(std::
            initializer_list <int>)" << std::
            endl;
    }

    A()
    {
        std::cout << "Inside A()" << std::
            endl;
    }
};

int main()
{
    A s1 = { 1.0, 2.0, 3.0 };
    A s2 = { 1, 2, 3 };
    A s3 = { };
}
```

Solution of Question 169

```
Inside A(std::initializer_list<double>)
Inside A(std::initializer_list<int>)
Inside A()
```

**** Question 170   initializer list and constructor

Explain how the following code works by simulating it using basic code snippets.

```
1 struct A
2 {
3     A( std :: initializer_list <double> v ) ;
4 };
5
6 A a{ 1 ,2 ,3 };
```

Solution of Question 170

The initialization will be implemented in a way roughly equivalent to this

```
1 const double a [3] = {double{1}, double{2},
      double{3}};
2 A a( std :: initializer_list <double>(a, a+3)) ;
```

assuming that the implementation can construct an *initializer_list* object with a pair of pointers.

*** Question 171   initializer list and array lifetime

What are the life-times of the arrays associated with the following expressions?

```
1 std :: vector<int> v1 = { 1, 2, 3 };
2
3 void f ()
4 {
5     std :: vector<int> v2{ 1, 2, 3 };
6
7     std :: initializer_list <int> i3 = { 1, 2, 3
          };
8 }
9
10 struct A
11 {
12     std :: initializer_list <int> i4 ;
13
14     A() : i4{ 1, 2, 3 } {}
15 };
```

Solution of Question 171

The array has the same lifetime as any other temporary object, except that initializing an *initializer_list* object from the array extends the lifetime of the array exactly like binding a reference to a temporary.

- For v1 and v2, the *initializer_list* object is a parameter in a function call, so the array created for { 1, 2, 3 } has full-expression lifetime.

- For i3, the *initializer_list* object is a variable, so the array persists for the lifetime of the variable.

- For i4, the *initializer_list* object is initialized in a constructor's initializer, so the array persists only until the constructor exits, and so any use of the elements of i4 after the constructor exits produces undefined behavior.

Chapter 6

Classes

** Question 172   trivial class

What is a *trivial class*?

Solution of Question 172

A trivially copyable class is a class that:

- has no non-trivial copy constructors,

- has no non-trivial move constructors,

- has no non-trivial copy assignment operators,

- has no non-trivial move assignment operators, and

- has a trivial destructor

A *trivial class* is a class that has a default constructor, has no non-trivial default constructors, and is trivially copyable. In particular, a trivially copyable or trivial class does not have virtual functions or virtual base classes.

** Question 173   this pointer

What is *this pointer*?

Solution of Question 173

In the body of a non-static member function, the keyword *this* is a *prvalue* expression whose value is the address of the object for which the function is called.

- The type of this in a member function of a class X is X*.

- If the member function is declared const, the type of this is const X*,

- if the member function is declared volatile, the type of this is volatile X*, and

- if the member function is declared const volatile, the type of this is const volatile X*.

Thus in a const member function, the object for which the function is called is accessed through a const access path.

*** Question 174   scope of static member

What is output of the program below?

Program 6.1: scope of static member

```
1 #include <iostream>
2
3 int g()
4 {
5     return 1;
6 }
7
8 struct X
9 {
10     static int g()
11     {
12         return 10;
13     }
14 };
15
16 struct Y : X
17 {
18     static int i;
19 };
20
21 int Y::i = g();
22
23 int main()
24 {
25     std::cout << Y::i << std::endl;
26 }
```

Solution of Question 174

It prints *10*. Because the code *int Y::i = g();* is equivalent *int Y::i = Y::g().*

*** Question 175   static member function

What are the properties of a static member function?

Solution of Question 175

- A static member function does not have a this pointer.

- A static member function can not be made virtual.

- There can not be a static and a non-static member function with the same name and the same parameter types.

- A static member function can not be declared const, volatile, or const volatile.

*** Question 176   static member data

What are the properties of a static member data?

Solution of Question 176

- A static data member is not part of the subobjects of a class. If a static data member is declared *thread_local* there is one copy of the member per thread. If a static data member is not declared *thread_local* there is one copy of the data member that is shared by all the objects of the class.

- The declaration of a static data member in its class definition is not a definition and may be of an incomplete type other than cv-qualified void. The definition for a static data member appears in a namespace scope enclosing the member's class definition. In the definition at namespace scope, the name of the static data member is qualified by its class name using the scope resolution operator, i.e., *:: operator*. The initializer expression in the definition of a static data member is in the scope of its class.

- Once the static data member has been defined, it exists even if no objects of its class have been created.

- If a non-volatile const static data member is of integral or enumeration type, its declaration in the class definition can specify a brace-or-equal-initializer in which every initializer-clause that is an assignment-expression is a constant expression. A static data member of literal type can be declared in the class definition with the constexpr specifier; if so, its declaration shall specify a brace-or-equal-initializer in which every initializer-clause that is an assignment-expression is a constant expression. In both these cases, the member may appear in constant expressions. The member is still be defined in a namespace scope if it is odr-used in the program and the namespace scope definition does not contain an initializer.

- There is exactly one definition of a static data member that is odr-used in a program. Unnamed classes and classes contained directly or indirectly within unnamed classes can not contain static data members.

- Static data members of a class in namespace scope have external linkage. A local class can not have static data members.

- Static data members are initialized and destroyed exactly like non-local variables.

- A static data member can not be mutable.

**** Question 177   member name lookup

In the program below, which x is modified by f.x = 0?

Program 6.2: member name lookup

```
1 struct A
2 {
3     int x;
4 };
5
6 struct B
7 {
8     float x;
9 };
10
11 struct C: A, B { };
12
13 struct D: virtual C { };
14
15 struct E: virtual C
16 {
17     char x;
```

```
18 };
19
20 struct F: D, E { };
21
22 int main ()
23 {
24     F f;
25     f.x = 0;
26 }
```

Solution of Question 177

Lookup finds *E::x*, because the A and B base subobjects of D are also base subobjects of E, so lookup in D is discarded in the first merge step.

** Question 178   member function lookup

In the program below, provide an implementation of the function f which returns the addition of the results of the respective functions of classes A and B.

```
1 struct A
2 {
3     int f ();
4 };
5
6 struct B
7 {
8     int f ();
9 };
10
11 struct C : A, B
12 {
13     int f ();
14 };
```

Solution of Question 178

```
1 struct A
2 {
3     int f ();
4 };
5
6 struct B
7 {
8     int f ();
9 };
10
```

```
11 struct C : A, B
12 {
13     int f () { return A :: f () + B :: f () ; }
14 };
```

*** Question 179   non-static member lookup

Review the program below.

Program 6.3: non-static member lookup

```
1 struct V
2 {
3     int v;
4 };
5
6 struct A
7 {
8     int a;
9     static int s;
10    enum { e };
11 };
12
13 struct B : A, virtual V { };
14 struct C : A, virtual V { };
15 struct D : B, C { };
16
17 void f (D* pd)
18 {
19     pd->v++;
20     pd->s++;
21     int i = pd->e;
22     pd->a++;
23 }
```

Solution of Question 179

Compiler error is:

```
member_name_lookup1.cpp:22:9:
error: non-static member 'a' found in multiple
    base-class subobjects of type 'A':
    struct D -> struct B -> struct A
    struct D -> struct C -> struct A
    pd->a++;
        ^
```

```
member_name_lookup1.cpp:8:9:
note: member found by ambiguous name lookup
    int a;
    ^
1 error generated.
```

- *pd->v++* is ok : only one v (virtual)

- *pd->s++* is also ok : only one s (static)

- *int i = pd->e* is also ok : only one e (enumerator)

- *pd->a++* is ambiguous because there are two *a*s in D

A static member, a nested type or an enumerator defined in a base class T can unambiguously be found even if an object has more than one base class subobject of type T. Two base class subobjects share the non-static member subobjects of their common virtual base classes.

*** Question 180   **member lookup and virtual base**

Review the program below.

Program 6.4: member lookup and virtual base

```
1 struct V
2 {
3     int f();
4     int x;
5 };
6
7 struct W
8 {
9     int g();
10     int y;
11 };
12
13 struct B : virtual V, W
14 {
15     int f(); int x;
16     int g(); int y;
17 };
18
19 struct C : virtual V, W { };
20
21 struct D : B, C { void glorp(); };
22
```

```
23 void D:: glorp ()
24 {
25     x++;
26     f () ;
27     y++;
28     g () ;
29 }
```

Solution of Question 180

Compiler error is:

```
virtual_base.cpp:27:5:
error: member 'y' found in multiple base classes of
      different types
    y++;
    ^

virtual_base.cpp:16:18:
note: member found by ambiguous name lookup
    int g(); int y;
                  ^

virtual_base.cpp:10:9:
note: member found by ambiguous name lookup
      int y;
          ^

virtual_base.cpp:28:5:
error: member 'g' found in multiple base classes of
      different types
    g();
    ^

virtual_base.cpp:16:9:
note: member found by ambiguous name lookup
    int g(); int y;
        ^

virtual_base.cpp:9:9:
note: member found by ambiguous name lookup
      int g();
          ^

2 errors generated.
```

In the function *void D::glorp()*:

- *x++* is ok because B::x hides V::x

- $f()$ is ok because B:f() hides V::f()

- $y++$ is ambiguous : B::y or C's W::y ?

- $g()$ is ambiguous : B::g() and C's W::g() ?

When virtual base classes are used, a hidden declaration can be reached along a path through the subobject lattice that does not pass through the hiding declaration. This is not an ambiguity. The identical use with non-virtual base classes is an ambiguity; in that case there is no unique instance of the name that hides all the others.

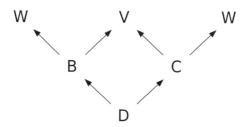

The names declared in V and the left-hand instance of W are hidden by those in B, but the names declared in the right-hand instance of W are not hidden at all.

*** Question 181   virtual function

What is the output of the program below?

Program 6.5: virtual function

```
1 #include <iostream>
2
3 struct A
4 {
5     virtual void f()
6     {
7         std::cout << "A::f()" << std::endl;
8     }
9 };
10
11 struct B : virtual A
12 {
```

```
13      virtual void f ()
14      {
15          std::cout << "B::f()" << std::endl;
16      }
17 };
18
19 struct C : B, virtual A
20 {
21      using A::f;
22 };
23
24 int main ()
25 {
26      C c;
27      c.f();
28      c.C::f();
29 }
```

Solution of Question 181

It prints

```
B::f()
A::f()
```

- *c.f()* calls *B::f* because of the final overrider

- *c.C::f()* calls *A::f* because of the using declaration.

Virtual functions support dynamic binding and object-oriented programming. A class that declares or inherits a virtual function is called a *polymorphic class.*

If a virtual member function *vf* is declared in a class *Base* and in a class *Derived*, derived directly or indirectly from *Base*, a member function *vf* with the same name, parameter-type-list, cv-qualification, and ref-qualifier (or absence of same) as *Base::vf* is declared, then *Derived::vf* is also virtual (whether or not it is so declared) and it overrides *Base::vf*.

For convenience we say that any virtual function overrides itself.

A virtual member function *C::vf* of a class object *S* is a final overrider unless the most derived class of which *S* is a base class subobject (if any) declares or inherits another member function that overrides *vf*.

In a derived class, if a virtual member function of a base class subobject has more than one final overrider the program is ill-formed.

**** Question 182   virtual function and hiding

Review the program below.

```
1 struct B
2 {
3     virtual void f();
4 };
5
6 struct D : B
7 {
8     void f(int);
9 };
10
11 struct D2 : D
12 {
13     void f();
14 };
```

Solution of Question 182

It is important to note that a virtual member function does not have to be visible to be overridden.

Here, the function *f(int)* in class *D* hides the virtual function *f()* in its base class *B*; *D::f(int)* is not a virtual function.

However, *f()* declared in class *D2* has the same name and the same parameter list as *B::f()*, and therefore is a virtual function that overrides the function *B::f()* even though *B::f()* is not visible in class *D2*.

** Question 183   virtual function and final

Review the program below.

Program 6.6: virtual function and final

```
1 struct B
2 {
3     virtual void f() const final;
4 };
5
6 struct D : B
7 {
```

```
8      void  f ()  const ;
9 };
```

Solution of Question 183

Compiler error is:

```
final_virtual.cpp:8:10:
error: declaration of 'f' overrides a
'final' function
    void f() const;
      ^

final_virtual.cpp:3:18:
note: overridden virtual function is here
    virtual void f() const final;
                  ^

1 error generated.
```

If a virtual function *f* in some class *B* is marked with the *virt-specifier final* and in a class *D* derived from *B*, a function *D::f* overrides *B::f*, the program is ill-formed.

*** Question 184   virtual function and override

Review the program below.

Program 6.7: virtual function and override

```
1 struct  B
2 {
3      virtual  void  f ( int ) ;
4 };
5
6 struct  D  :  B
7 {
8      virtual  void  f ( long )  override ;
9      virtual  void  f ( int )  override ;
10 };
```

Solution of Question 184

Compiler error is:

```
override_virtual.cpp:8:18:
error: 'f' marked 'override' but does not override
      any member functions
      virtual void f(long) override;
                   ^
1 error generated.
```

If a virtual function is marked with the *virt-specifier override*
and does not override a member function of a base class, the
program is ill-formed.

**** Question 185   **access default template argument**

Review the program below.

Program 6.8: access default template argument
```
1 class B { };
2
3 template <class T>
4 class C
5 {
6 protected:
7     typedef T TT;
8 };
9
10 template <class U, class V = typename U::TT>
11 class D : public U { };
12
13 int main()
14 {
15     D <C<B> >* d;
16 }
```

Solution of Question 185

Compiler error is:

```
default_template_argument.cpp:10:42:
error: 'TT' is a protected member of 'C<B>'
template <class U, class V = typename U::TT>
                                         ^
default_template_argument.cpp:15:5:
note: in instantiation of default argument
      for 'D<C<B> >' required here
```

```
    D <C<B> >* d;
      ^~~~~~~~~
default_template_argument.cpp:7:15:
note: declared protected here
    typedef T TT;
            ^

1 error generated.
```

The names in a default template-argument have their access
checked in the context in which they appear rather than at any
points of use of the default template-argument.

** Question 186   friend constructor/destructor

Is the following program valid ?

```
1 class Y
2 {
3     friend char* X::foo(int);
4     friend X::X(char);
5     friend X::~X();
6 };
```

Solution of Question 186

Yes.

When a friend declaration refers to an overloaded name or operator, only the function specified by the parameter types becomes a friend. A member function of a class X can be a friend
of a class Y.

Hence constructors and destructors too can be friends.

**** Question 187   access to virtual function

Is the following program valid ? If yes, what is its output ?

Program 6.9: access to virtual function

```
1 #include <iostream>
2
3 struct B
4 {
5     virtual void f()
6     {
7         std::cout << "B::f()" << std::endl;
8     }
9 };
```

```
10
11 struct D : B
12 {
13 private :
14     void f ()
15     {
16         std :: cout << "D:: f ()" << std :: endl;
17     }
18 };
19
20 int main ()
21 {
22     D d;
23     B* pb = &d;
24     pb->f () ;
25 }
```

Solution of Question 187

Yes.

It prints

```
D::f()
```

The access rules for a virtual function are determined by its declaration and are not affected by the rules for a function that later overrides it.

** Question 188   const/volatile constructor

Can a constructor be declared *const, volatile* or *const volatile* ?

Solution of Question 188

No.

A constructor can not be declared *const, volatile* or *const volatile*. *const* and *volatile* semantics are not applied on an object under construction. They come into effect when the constructor for the most derived object ends.

*** Question 189   new and dangling reference

Review the program.

Program 6.10: new and dangling reference

```
1 #include <utility >
```

```
2
3 struct A
4 {
5     int i;
6     const std::pair<int,int>& p;
7 };
8
9 int main()
10 {
11     A * p = new A{ 1, {2, 3} };
12 }
```

Solution of Question 189

It results into a compilation error:

```
dangling_ref_new.cpp:11:24: error:
reference to type 'const std::pair<int, int>'
    could not bind to an rvalue of type 'int'
    A * p = new A{ 1, {2, 3} };
                  ^

1 error generated.
```

A temporary bound to a reference in a new-initializer persists until the completion of the full-expression containing the new-initializer. Here, the line 11 creates a dangling reference.

*** Question 190   user defined conversion

Is the following user defined conversions allowed?

Program 6.11: user defined conversion

```
1 struct X
2 {
3     operator int();
4 };
5
6 struct Y
7 {
8     operator X();
9 };
10
11 int main()
12 {
13     Y a;
14     int b = a;
```

```
15      int  c = X(a);
16 }
```

Solution of Question 190

It results into a compilation error:

```
conversion.cpp:14:9:
error: no viable conversion from 'Y' to 'int'
    int b = a;
        ^   ~

conversion.cpp:8:5: note: candidate function
    operator X();
    ^

1 error generated.
```

At most one user-defined conversion (constructor or conversion function) is implicitly applied to a single value.

- *int b = a;* is an error: a.operator X().operator int() is not tried here.

- *int c = X(a);* is fine: a.operator X().operator int() is applied.

** Question 191   conversion by constructor

Review the program.

Program 6.12: conversion by constructor

```
1 struct A
2 {
3      A(int);
4      A(const char*, int =0);
5      A(int, int);
6 };
7
8 void f(A arg)
9 {
10     A a = 1;
11     A b = "Lin";
12     a = 2;
13     f(3);
14     f({1, 2});
15 }
```

Solution of Question 191

This is a valid code. A constructor declared without the function-specifier *explicit* specifies a conversion from the types of its parameters to the type of its class. Such a constructor is called a *converting constructor*.

- *A a = 1* is same as *A a = A(1)*

- *A b = "Lin"* is same as *A b = A("Lin", 0)*;

- *a = 2* is same as *a = A(2)*

- *f(3)* is equivalent to *f(A(3))*

- *f({1, 2})* is equivalent to calling *f(A(1, 2))*

** Question 192   conversion operator

Will all three calls depicted below will invoke the supplied conversion constructor?

```
1 struct A
2 {
3     operator int () ;
4 };
5
6 void f (A a)
7 {
8     int i = int (a) ;
9     i = (int)a ;
10    i = a ;
11 }
```

Solution of Question 192

Yes, in all three cases the value assigned will be converted by *A::operator int()*.

*** Question 193   destructor

What is the output of the program below?

Program 6.13: destructor

```
1 #include <iostream>
2
3 struct B
4 {
```

```cpp
5       virtual ~B()
6       {
7               std::cout << "B::~B()" << std::endl;
8       }
9  };
10
11 struct D : B
12 {
13      ~D()
14      {
15              std::cout << "D::~D()" << std::endl;
16      }
17 };
18
19 int main()
20 {
21      D d;
22      typedef B B1;
23
24      B* bptr = &d;
25
26      d.B::~B();
27
28      bptr->~B();
29
30      bptr->~B1();
31
32      bptr->B1::~B();
33
34      bptr->B1::~B1();
35 }
```

Solution of Question 193

```
B::~B()
B::~D()
B::~D()
B::~B()
B::~B()
D::~D()
B::~B()
```

- *d.B:: B();* calls B's destructor

- *bptr-> B();* calls D's destructor

- *bptr-> B1();* calls D's destructor

- *bptr->B1:: B();* calls B's destructor

- *bptr->B1:: B1();* calls B's destructor

*** Question 194   explicit call of destructor

Demonstrate an explicit call of destructor.

Solution of Question 194

Explicit calls of destructors are rarely needed. One use of such calls is for objects placed at specific addresses using a new-expression with the placement option. Such use of explicit placement and destruction of objects can be necessary to cope with dedicated hardware resources and for writing memory management facilities. For example,

```
1 void* operator new(std::size_t, void* p)
2 {
3     return p;
4 }
5
6 struct X
7 {
8     X(int);
9     ~X();
10 };
11
12 void f(X* p);
13
14 void g() // rare, specialized use:
15 {
16     char* buf = new char[sizeof(X)];
17     X* p = new(buf) X(222); // use buf[] and
                    initialize
18     f(p);
19     p->X::~X(); // cleanup
20 }
```

*** Question 195   destructor for any type

Is this a valid code ?

```
1 typedef int I;
2 I* p;
3 p->I::~I();
```

Solution of Question 195

Yes.

The notation for explicit call of a destructor can be used for any scalar type name. Allowing this makes it possible to write code without having to know if a destructor exists for a given type.

** Question 196   signature of deallocation function

Provide the signature(s) of deallocation function(s) for a given class A.

Solution of Question 196

```
1 class A
2 {
3     void operator delete(void*);
4     void operator delete[](void*, std::size_t
          );
5 };
```

Any deallocation function for a class *A* is a static member (even if not explicitly declared static).

*** Question 197   delete and virtual

What is the output of the program?

Program 6.14: delete and virtual

```
1 #include <iostream>
2
3 struct B
4 {
5     virtual ~B()
6     {
7         std::cout << "B::~B()" << std::endl;
8     }
9
10    void operator delete(void*, std::size_t)
11    {
12        std::cout << "B::operator delete" <<
             std::endl;
13    }
14 };
15
16 struct D : B
17 {
18     void operator delete(void*)
```

```
19        {
20            std :: cout << "D:: operator␣delete" <<
                  std :: endl ;
21        }
22 } ;
23
24 int  main ( )
25 {
26      B*  bp = new D;
27      delete  bp ;
28 }
```

Solution of Question 197

It prints:

```
B::~B()
D::operator delete
```

Since member allocation and deallocation functions are static
they cannot be virtual. However, when the cast-expression of a
delete-expression refers to an object of class type, because the
deallocation function actually called is looked up in the scope of
the class that is the dynamic type of the object, if the destructor
is virtual, the effect is the same.

Here, storage for the non-array object of class D is deallocated
by *D::operator delete()*, due to the virtual destructor, i.e., *delete
bp* calls *D::operator delete(void*)*.

Please note that access to the deallocation function is checked
statically. Hence, even though a different one might actually be
executed, the statically visible deallocation function is required
to be accessible. If *B::operator delete()* had been *private* above,
the delete expression would have been ill-formed then.

**** Question 198   base class initializer

Review the program ?

Program 6.15: base class initializer

```
1 struct A
2 {
3      A ( ) ;
4 } ;
5
```

```
6  struct B: virtual A { };
7
8  struct C: A, B
9  {
10     C();
11 };
12
13 C::C(): A() { }
```

Solution of Question 198

Compiler error is:

```
mem_initializer.cpp:13:9: error:
base class initializer 'A' names both a direct
base class and an inherited virtual base class
C::C(): A() { }
        ^

1 error generated.
```

If a *mem-initializer-id* is ambiguous because it designates both a direct non-virtual base class and an inherited virtual base class, the *mem-initializer* is ill-formed.

Here, *C::C(): A()* is ill-formed : which A ?

*** Question 199   pack expansion and initializer

Is this program valid one ?

```
1  template<class ... Mixins>
2  class X : public Mixins ...
3  {
4  public:
5      X(const Mixins&... mixins)
6      :
7      Mixins(mixins) ... { }
8  };
```

Solution of Question 199

Yes. A *mem-initializer* followed by an ellipsis is a *pack expansion* that initializes the base classes specified by a pack expansion in the *base-specifier-list* for the class.

*** Question 200   non-trivial constructor

Is this program valid one ?

```
1 struct W { int j; };
2 struct X : public virtual W { };
3 struct Y
4 {
5     int *p;
6     X x;
7
8     Y() : p(&x.j) { }
9 };
```

Solution of Question 200

No.

For an object with a non-trivial constructor, referring to any non-static member or base class of the object before the constructor begins execution results in undefined behavior.

For an object with a non-trivial destructor, referring to any non-static member or base class of the object after the destructor finishes execution results in undefined behavior.

Here, *Y() : p(&x.j)* will lead to undefined behavior because *x* is not yet constructed.

**** Question 201   initializer and this

Review the program.

Program 6.16: initializer and this

```
1 struct A { };
2
3 struct B : virtual A { };
4
5 struct C : B { };
6
7 struct D : virtual A
8 {
9     D(A*);
10 };
11
12 struct X
13 {
14     X(A*);
15 };
16
17 struct E : C, D, X
18 {
19     E() : D(this), X(this) { }
20 };
```

Solution of Question 201

To explicitly or implicitly convert a pointer (a glvalue) referring to an object of class X to a pointer (reference) to a direct or indirect base class B of X, the construction of X and the construction of all of its direct or indirect bases that directly or indirectly derive from B should have started and the destruction of these classes should not have completed, otherwise the conversion results in undefined behavior.

To form a pointer to (or access the value of) a direct non-static member of an object obj, the construction of obj should have started and its destruction should not have completed, otherwise the computation of the pointer value (or accessing the member value) results in undefined behavior.

Here $E() : D(this)$ has undefined behavior because upcast from E^* to A^* might use path $E* \Rightarrow D* \Rightarrow A*$ but D is not constructed, $D((C^*)this)$ is defined, $E* \Rightarrow C*$ is defined because $E()$ has started, and $C* \Rightarrow A*$ is defined because C is fully constructed.

Whereas $X(this)$ is defined because upon construction of X, $C/B/D/A$ sublattice is fully constructed.

*** Question 202   dynamic_cast and construction

Review the program.

Program 6.17: dynamic_cast and construction

```
1 #include <typeinfo>
2 struct V
3 {
4     virtual void f();
5 };
6
7 struct A : virtual V { };
8
9 struct B : virtual V
10 {
11     B(V*, A*);
12 };
13
14 struct D : A, B
15 {
16     D() : B((A*)this, this) { }
17 };
18
```

```
19 B::B(V*  v,  A*  a)
20 {
21       typeid(*this);
22
23       typeid(*v);
24
25       typeid(*a);
26
27       dynamic_cast<B*>(v);
28
29       dynamic_cast<B*>(a);
30 }
```

Solution of Question 202

dynamic_casts can be used during construction or destruction.

When a *dynamic_cast* is used in a constructor (including the *mem-initializer* or *brace-or-equal-initializer* for a non-static data member) or in a destructor, or used in a function called (directly or indirectly) from a constructor or destructor, if the operand of the *dynamic_cast* refers to the object under construction or destruction, this object is considered to be a most derived object that has the type of the constructor or destructor's class.

If the operand of the *dynamic_cast* refers to the object under construction or destruction and the static type of the operand is not a pointer to or object of the constructor or destructor's own class or one of its bases, the *dynamic_cast* results in undefined behavior.

Here,

- *typeid(*this)* is *type_info* for B.

- *typeid(*v)* is well-defined: *v has type V, a base of B yields *type_info* for B.

- *typeid(*a)* has undefined behavior: type A not a base of B

- *dynamic_cast<B*>(v)* is well-defined: v of type V*, V base of B results in B*.

- *dynamic_cast<B*>(a)* has undefined behavior, a has type A*, A not a base of B.

** Question 203   inheriting constructors

Enlist the constructors available in *D1* and *D2*.

```
struct B1
{
    B1(int);
};

struct B2
{
    B2(int = 13, int = 42);
};

struct D1 : B1
{
    using B1::B1;
};

struct D2 : B2
{
    using B2::B2;
};
```

Solution of Question 203

The candidate set of inherited constructors in D1 for B1 is

- B1(const B1&)

- B1(B1&&)

- B1(int)

The set of constructors present in D1 is

- D1(), implicitly-declared default constructor, ill-formed if odr-used

- D1(const D1&), implicitly-declared copy constructor, not inherited

- D1(D1&&), implicitly-declared move constructor, not inherited

- D1(int), implicitly-declared inheriting constructor

The candidate set of inherited constructors in D2 for B2 is

- B2(const B2&)

- B2(B2&&)

- B2(int = 13, int = 42)

- B2(int = 13)

- B2()

The set of constructors present in D2 is

- D2(), implicitly-declared default constructor, not inherited

- D2(const D2&), implicitly-declared copy constructor, not inherited

- D2(D2&&), implicitly-declared move constructor, not inherited

- D2(int, int), implicitly-declared inheriting constructor

- D2(int), implicitly-declared inheriting constructor

*** Question 204   hiding

Review the program.

Program 6.18: hiding

```
1 struct B
2 {
3     int f(int);
4 };
5
6 struct D : B
7 {
8     int f(const char*);
9 };
10
11 void h(D* pd)
12 {
13     pd->f(1);
14     pd->B::f(1);
15     pd->f("Ben");
16 }
```

Solution of Question 204

Compiler error is:

```
hiding.cpp: In function 'void h(D*)':
hiding.cpp:13:12: error: invalid conversion from
'int' to 'const char*' [-fpermissive]
    pd->f(1);
          ^
hiding.cpp:8:9: error:    initializing argument 1
of 'int D::f(const char*)' [-fpermissive]
    int f(const char*);
        ^
```

A function member of a derived class is not in the same scope
as a function member of the same name in a base class. Here
$D{::}f(const\ char^*)$ hides $B{::}f(int)$ rather than overloading it.
Hence the call $pd{-}{>}f(1)$ is in error.

*** Question 205   hiding operators

Review the program.

Program 6.19: hiding operators

```
1 struct A { };
2
3 void operator + (A, A);
4
5 struct B
6 {
7     void operator + (B);
8     void f ();
9 };
10
11 A a;
12
13 void B::f ()
14 {
15     operator+ (a,a);
16     a + a;
17 }
```

Solution of Question 205

Compiler error is:

```
operators.cpp:15:18: error: too many arguments to
function call, expected 1,
      have 2
    operator+ (a,a);
    ~~~~~~~~~     ^

operators.cpp:7:5: note: 'operator+' declared here
    void operator + (B);
    ^

1 error generated.
```

The lookup rules for operators in expressions are different than the lookup rules for operator function names in a function call.

Here *operator+ (a,a)* is in error because global operator is hidden by the member operator. Where the expression *a + a* is ok as it calls the global *operator+*.

Chapter 7

Templates

** Question 206   non type template parameters

Which of the following class template declarations is valid?

```
1 template<double d> class X;
2 template<double* pd> class Y;
3 template<double& rd> class Z;
```

Solution of Question 206

A non-type template-parameter can not be declared to have floating point, class, or void type.

Hence *template<double d> class X* is invalid, the rest are ok.

** Question 207   default template parameters

Review the program.

```
1 template<class T1, class T2 = int> class A;
2 template<class T1 = int, class T2> class A;
```

Solution of Question 207

The set of default template-arguments available for use with a template declaration or definition is obtained by merging the default arguments from the definition (if in scope) and all declarations in scope in the same way default function arguments are.

Hence the program is equivalent to

```
1 template<class T1 = int, class T2 = int>
    class A;
```

*** Question 208   template and template-id

Review the program.

```
 1 template <class T>
 2 struct A
 3 {
 4     void f(int);
 5     template <class U>
 6     void f(U);
 7 };
 8
 9 template <class T>
10 void f(T t)
11 {
12     A<T> a;
13     a.template f<>(t);
14     a.template f(t);
15 }
16
17 template <class T>
18 struct B
19 {
20     template <class T2>
21     struct C { };
22 };
23
24 template <class T, template <class X> class
       TT = T::template C>
25 struct D { };
26
27 D<b<int> > db;
```

Solution of Question 208

a.template f<>(t); is ok : it calls the template, but
a.template f(t); is in error because it is not a template-id.

default template parameter of *struct D* is alos ok because
T::template C names a class template.

**** Question 209   template argument and type-id

What is the output of the program?

Program 7.1: template argument and type-id
```
1 #include <iostream>
2
3 template<class T>
4 void f()
```

```
5 {
6      std :: cout  <<  "template<class_T>_void_f"
           <<  std :: endl ;
7 }
8
9 template<int  I>
10 void  f ()
11 {
12     std :: cout  <<  "template<int_I>_void_f"  <<
           std :: endl ;
13 }
14
15 int  main ()
16 {
17     f<int () >() ;
18 }
```

Solution of Question 209

It prints

```
template<class T> void f
```

In a template-argument, an ambiguity between a *type-id* and
an expression is resolved to a *type-id*, regardless of the form of
the corresponding template-parameter.

Hence *f<int()>()* calls the first *f()* because *int()* is a type-id.

*** Question 210   explicit specialization vs static

Is this program valid ?

```
1 template <class  T> struct  A
2 {
3      static  int  i [] ;
4 };
5
6 template <class  T> int  A<T>:: i [4] ;
7
8 template <> int  A<int >:: i [] = { 1 };
```

Solution of Question 210

Yes.

An explicit specialization of a static data member declared as
an array of unknown bound can have a different bound from its
definition, if any.

** Question 211   virtual member function template

Review the program.

Program 7.2: virtual member function template

```
1 template <class T>
2 struct A
3 {
4     template <class U>
5     virtual void f (U);
6 };
```

Solution of Question 211

Compiler error is:

```
virtual_template.cpp:5:5: error:
'virtual' can not be specified on member
    function templates
    virtual void f(U);
    ^~~~~~~
1 error generated.
```

A member function template can not be virtual.

*** Question 212   override virtual and template

Which of the following member function overrides *B::f(int)*?

```
1 class B
2 {
3     virtual void f (int);
4 };
5
6 class D : public B
7 {
8     template <class T>
9     void f (T);
10
11     void f (int i)
12     {
13         f<>(i);
14     }
15 };
```

Solution of Question 212

A specialization of a member function template does not override a virtual function from a base class.

Hence *template <class T> void f(T)* does not override *B::f(int)*.

void f(int i) is the overriding function that calls the template instantiation.

*** Question 213   parameter pack

What is a *template parameter pack* and *function parameter pack?*

Solution of Question 213

A *template parameter pack* is a template parameter that accepts zero or more template arguments. For example:

```
1 template<class ... Types> struct Tuple { };
2 Tuple<> t0; // Types contains no arguments
3 Tuple<int> t1; // Types contains one argument
    : int
4 Tuple<int, float> t2; // Types contains two
    arguments : int and float
5 Tuple<0> error; // error : 0 is not a type
```

A *function parameter pack* is a function parameter that accepts zero or more function arguments. For example:

```
1 template<class ... Types> void f(Types ...
    args);
2 f(); // args contains no arguments
3 f(1); // args contains one argument: int
4 f(2, 1.0); // args contains two arguments:
    int and double
```

*** Question 214   alias template

What is an *alias template* ?

Solution of Question 214

A template-declaration in which the declaration is an alias-declaration declares the identifier to be a *alias template*. An *alias template* is a name for a family of types. The name of the *alias template* is a template-name.

When a template-id refers to the specialization of an alias template, it is equivalent to the associated type obtained by substitution of its template-arguments for the template-parameters in the type-id of the alias template.

For example

```
1 template<class T> struct Alloc { */ ... */ };
2 template<class T> using Vec = vector<T, Alloc
    <T>>;
3 Vec<int> v; // same as vector<int, Alloc<int
    >> v;
```

Please note that an alias template name is never deduced.

Chapter 8

Standard Library

*** Question 215   constraint class

Write a constraint class *HasEqual* that checks for the existence
of the == operator.

Solution of Question 215

```
1 template<typename T, typename U>
2 struct HasEqual<T, U>
3 {
4     HasEqual() { auto p = constraints; }
5
6     static void constraints(T x, U y)
7     {
8         x == y;
9     }
10 };
```

The *HasEqual* constructor forces the instantiation of the static
constraints member function by declaring a pointer to the function. This function implements a set of valid expressions for the
objects introduced by its formal parameters.

The body of this constraints function contains a single statement that forces a lookup on an appropriate == for types of T
and U. If no such operator can be found, instantiation will fail,
and the compiler emits the appropriate error message.

The result of the expression is unconstrained here.

**** Question 216   reusing constraint class

Reuse the above constraint class *HasEqual* to implement the concept class *EqualityComparable*.

Solution of Question 216

Constraint classes can be reused through either inheritance or composition.

```
1 template<typename T>
2 struct EqualityComparable : HasEqual<T, T>
3 {
4     EqualityComparable ()
5     {
6         auto p = constraints;
7     }
8
9     static void constraints (T x, T y)
10    {
11        Convertible<decltype (x == y), bool
            >{};
12
13        Convertible<decltype (x != y), bool
            >{};
14    }
15 };
```

The inheritance of *HasEqual* causes the constraint to be checked before the constraints in the *EqualityComparable* constraint class by virtue of the initialization order. The *EqualityComparable* class applies additional constraints within its body.

Here, the *Convertible* constraint is written as an explicit initialization of a temporary object. This checks if the result of an expression (the *decltype* operator returns the type of an expression) can be converted to the specified type, here, *bool*.

A similar requirement is made for !=. *Convertible* is defined as:

```
1 template<typename T, typename U>
2 struct Convertible
3 {
4     Convertible ()
5     {
6         static_assert (std :: is_convertible <T,
            U>:: value , "Not␣convertible");
7     }
8 };
```

The constraint is implemented by statically asserting the *std::is_convertible* type trait. A *type trait* is a class template that evaluates some property of its type arguments. The nested value contains the result of the evaluation. A constraints function is not needed since the trait can be evaluated without introducing objects.

*** Question 217   type traits

Provide an implementation of a type trait *is_same* as a class template such that *is_same<X, Y>::value* is only true when X and Y name the same type. The resulting value should be a constant expression that can be evaluated by the compiler in contexts such as a *static_assert*.

Solution of Question 217

```
1 template<typename T, typename U>
2 struct is_same
3 {
4     static constexpr bool value = false;
5 };
6
7 template<typename T>
8 struct is_same<T, T>
9 {
10    static constexpr bool value = true;
11 };
```

The primary template (the first declaration) defines the result when X and Y are different types. The specialization defines the result when the template arguments are the same.

*** Question 218   advance and next

Provide an implementation of the STL algorithm *advance* for input and forward iterators and then implement an iterator utility *next* using *advance* algorithm.

Solution of Question 218

```
1 template<typename Iter>
2 void advance(Iter& first, int n)
3 {
4     while(n > 0)
5     {
6         ++first;
7         --n;
8     }
9 }
10
```

```
11 template<typename Iter>
12 Iter next(Iter i, int n = 1)
13 {
14     advance(i, n);
15     return i;
16 }
```

*** Question 219   custom iota

Customize the increment/decrement part of the STL algorithm *iota*.

Solution of Question 219

Overload iota for custom increment step:

```
1 template <typename ForwardIterator, typename
      T>
2 void iota( ForwardIterator first ,
      ForwardIterator last ,
3 T value , T step = 1 )
4 {
5     for ( ; first != last; ++first , value +=
          step )
6     *first = value;
7 }
8
9 //Usage :
10 std::vector<int> vint (5);
11 std::vector<int> v_expected = {5, 10, 15, 20,
      25};
12 iota ( vint.begin() , vint.end() , //destination
      range
13 5, // start value
14 5);// increment by 5
15
16 assert(std::equal(vint.begin(),vint.end(),
      v_expected.begin())) ;
```

Overloading iota with step size as an additional argument requires changing the implementation along-with the established interface, which may not be viable in every situation. On the other hand, we can easily achieve the same output with overloading pre-increment operator as follows:

```
1 template <typename InitialValue , typename
      StepSize>
2 struct step_helper
3 {
```

```
4      step_helper(InitialValue val, StepSize
          step)
5      : _val(val), _step(step) {}
6
7      step_helper & operator++()
8      {
9          _val += _step; return *this;
10     }
11
12     operator InitialValue() { return _val; }
13
14 private:
15     InitialValue _val;
16     const StepSize _step;
17 };
18
19 template<typename InitialValue, typename
          StepSize = InitialValue>
20 step_helper<InitialValue, StepSize>
21 step(InitialValue val, StepSize s = 1)
22 {
23     return step_helper<InitialValue, StepSize
          >(val, s);
24 }
25
26 // Usage : custom increment is 10
27 std::array<int, 5> arr;
28 std::array<int, 5> arr_res = {5, 15, 25, 35,
          45};
29 std::iota(arr.begin(), arr.end(), step(5, 10)
          );
30 assert(std::equal(arr.begin(), arr.end(),
          arr_res.begin()));
```

*** Question 220   all_of algorithm

Implement the STL algorithm *all_of* using *find_if_not* and *find_if*.

Solution of Question 220

```
1 template<typename InputIterator, typename
          Predicate>
2 inline bool
3 all_of(InputIterator first, InputIterator
          last, Predicate pred)
4 {
5      return last == std::find_if_not(first,
          last, pred);
```

```
6 }
7
8 template<typename InputIterator , typename
    Predicate>
9 inline bool
10 all_of(InputIterator first , InputIterator
    last , Predicate pred)
11 {
12     return last == std :: find_if(first , last ,
        std :: not1(pred));
13 }
```

*** Question 221   is_partitioned algorithm

Implement the STL algorithm *is_partitioned* with the interface

```
1 template<typename InputIterator , typename
    Predicate>
2 bool is_partitioned(InputIterator first ,
    InputIterator last , Predicate p);
```

It returns true if

- if [first, last) is partitioned by the unary predicate p, i.e. if all elements that satisfy p appear before those that do not. Or,

- if [first, last) is empty.

In other words, all the items in the sequence that satisfy the predicate are at the beginning of the sequence.

Solution of Question 221

There are two phases of this algorithm:

1. Find the first occurrence of the element which does not satisfy the predicate. The algorithm *std::find_if_not* perfectly fits the bill here.

2. None of the elements should satisfy the predicate starting from the element found above. *std::none_of* can be used to get this job done easily.

```
1 template<typename InputIterator , typename
    Predicate>
2 bool is_partitioned(InputIterator first ,
    InputIterator last ,
```

```
3 Predicate p)
4 {
5      first = std::find_if_not(first , last ,
            pred);
6      return std::none_of(first , last , pred);
7 }
```

or

```
1 template<typename InputIterator , typename
      Predicate>
2 bool is_partitioned(InputIterator first ,
      InputIterator last ,
3 Predicate p)
4 {
5      while(first != last && pred(*first))
6      ++first ;
7
8      while(first != last && pred(*first))
9      ++first ;
10
11     return (first == last);
12 }
```

Index

Printed in Great Britain
by Amazon.co.uk, Ltd.,
Marston Gate.